1945

THE NEWS

THE EVENTS

AND

THE LIVES

OF 1945

WILLIAM DEAN & ELIZABETH ABSALOM

D'AZUR PUBLISHING

Published by D'Azur Publishing 2024
D'Azur Publishing is a Division of D'Azur Limited

Copyright © D'Azur Publishing 2024

William Dean and Elizabeth Absalom have asserted his rights under the Copyright, Design and Patents Act 1988 to be identified as the author of this work.

The language, phrases and terminology within this book are as written at the time of the news reports during the year covered and convey and illustrate the sentiments at that time, even though modern society may find some words inappropriate. The news reports are taken from internationally recognised major newspapers and other sources of the year in question. The language does not represent any personal view of the author or publisher.

First published in Great Britain in 2024 by D'Azur Limited
Contact: info@d-azur.com Visit www.d-azur.com
ISBN 9798325923227

ACKNOWLEDGEMENTS
The publisher wishes to acknowledge the following people and sources:

Research Amanda Dean; British Newspaper Archive; The Times Archive; Cover Malcolm Watson; p7 Good Words Books; p12 (March) Campaign for Nuclear Disarmament; p14 Swinging Radio England; p15 Adam Cuerden; p16 By Ivan - State Library of New South Wales; p17 Political and communist; p17 The Labour Party; p27 45Worlds.com; p31 Visit Scotland; p35 Mariano C; p39 North Altlantic Aviation Museum; 41 (Turkey) Tyler Jamieson Moulton; p41 (Soldiers) The Gurkha Museum: p43 By SAC Neil Chapman (Fighters); By Photo: Air Historical Branch-RAF/MOD (Bomber); Alan Wilson (bi plane); p49 London Coins; p53 Bruno Guerrero; p61 (crowds) Mrjspence; p67 Bundesarchiv, Bild 101I-729-0001-23 / Meister / CC-BY-SA 3; p77 Blackburn Library; p89 Donna D; rollercollin; GrandPanjandrum; p95 Malcolm Watson; p95 Image by NakNakNak from Pixabay; p99 commandoveterans.org; p101 Notts Heritage; p105 P&O; p109 By RuthAS - Own work; p111 The Shipwrights Company; p117 RAF Museum; p123 Florence D;

Whilst we have made every effort to contact copyright holders, should we have made any omission, please contact us so that we can make the appropriate acknowledgement.

CONTENTS

1945 HIGHLIGHTS

Monarch: King George VI Prime Minister: Sir Winston Churchill (to 26th July) Clement Attlee (from 26th July)

Until May 1945, Winston Churchill's inspiring and resolute leadership was guiding the country through yet another year of wartime rationing and austerity where virtually every household item was either in short supply and had to be queued for or was unobtainable. But there was a huge sense of optimism that the war was won and great celebrations when Germany surrendered on 8th May and Japan on 2nd September.

Queuing for bread (above).
Pre fabricated house (below).

Planning was well under way for the future and thousands of temporary houses were being provided for the bombed out. In July, Winston Churchill, so popular as leader during the war, was ousted by a landslide in the General Election by the Labour Party, with their emphasis on social reform, full employment, affordable housing, social security and health care for all. The community spirit engendered by the war had given a universal feeling that, after victory, the country could not go back to pre-war social conditions.

FAMOUS PEOPLE WHO WERE BORN IN 1945

6th Jan: Rod Stewart, rock singer
25th Feb: Elkie Brooks, singer
30th Mar: Eric Clapton, rock guitarist
20th Apr: Alistair Cooke, historian and author
19th May: Pete Townshend, rock guitarist
17th Jun: Ken Livingstone, politician
10th July: Virginia Wade, tennis player
31st Aug: Van Morrison, singer-songwriter
26th Sep: Bryan Ferry, pop rock singer

FAMOUS PEOPLE WHO DIED IN 1945

31st Jan: Les Adams, rugby league player
20th Mar: Lord Alfred Douglas, poet and former lover of Oscar Wilde
26th Mar: David Lloyd George, former P. Minister
29th Mar: Jack Agazarian, spy
7th Apr: Elizabeth Bibesco, writer and socialite
11th Apr: Cecil Griffiths, athlete.
27th Jul: Alfred Dobbs, politician
31st Oct: Henry Ainley, actor

JANUARY Following the death of William Temple, Geoffrey Fisher was appointed the new Archbishop of Canterbury.

FEBRUARY Winston Churchill joined the heads of government of the US and Soviet Union at Yalta to discuss the postwar reorganization of Germany and Europe after the war.

MARCH The last 'Doodle Bug' attack on the UK takes place. The last enemy action of any kind on British soil occurs when one lands at Datchworth, Herts. There are no fatalities or injuries.

APRIL Robert McIntyre is the first Scottish National Party member to be elected to the British Parliament. Sybil Campbell is appointed the first woman to become a professional judge in the UK.

MAY Winston Churchill forms a "caretaker" Conservative government whilst awaiting a general election. This officially ends the wartime Coalition.

JUNE The Family Allowances Act providing payments to families with children is passed and demobilisation of the wartime troops begins.

JULY There is a three-week delay in counting the votes in the general election as certain areas did not vote until after their annual "Wakes Weeks" holidays and also so that votes from servicemen still overseas could be counted.

AUGUST The end of World War II is celebrated when the Japanese surrender but in parliament, Winston Churchill warns of an "Iron Curtain" descending across Europe.

SEPTEMBER This month sees the end of Press censorship and also of the Lend-Lease arrangement with the US.

OCTOBER Piccadilly Circus tube station is the first one to be lit by fluorescent lights.

NOVEMBER Fascist and Nazi collaborator, John Amery, son of British statesman, Leo Amery, is found guilty of treason and sentenced to hang.

DECEMBER The Jodrell Bank Observatory in Cheshire is established by Bernard Lovell. Britain sees bananas for the first time since the beginning of the war.

FILMS AND ARTS

Elizabeth Taylor is propelled to stardom at 12 years of age when **National Velvet** with Mickey Rooney and Donald Crisp is released in the US and becomes an instant critical and commercial success.

The **Lost Weekend** starring Ray Mill and and Jane Wyman, a story of an alcoholic writer, was nominated for seven Academy Awards and won four. Celia Johnson and Trevor Howard captivated British audiences with **Brief Encounter**, the romantic drama of a married woman, whose conventional life becomes increasingly complicated after a chance meeting at a railway station with a married stranger whom she subsequently falls in love with.

The London theatre remained important for the British people during 1945 providing an escape from post war austerity and now that it was safe, the curtain went back up everywhere. The **Windmill Theatre** proudly boasted "Never Closed, Never Clothed". The **Ivy Benson Big Band** the first all-female swing band led by Leeds-born Ivy Benson, was enormously popular and Ivor Novello's **Perchance to Dream**, which opened at the Hippodrome, gave us his wartime popular tune, **We'll Gather Lilacs**.

As well as the news, the BBC was still our main home entertainment with **Music While You Work, Desert Island Discs** and **Family Favourites**.

1945 THE YEAR

Born in 1945, you were one of 48.7 million people living in Britain and your life expectancy *then* was about 64.1 years. You were one of the 16 births per 1,000 population and you had a 6.5% chance of dying as an infant, most likely from an infectious disease such as polio, diphtheria, tetanus, whooping cough, measles, mumps or rubella. Although the war had ended, the country was living under unprecedented regulations governing every aspect of life, no-one in your family would be 'untouched' by the war and you would be reliant on rationing and ration books for some years to come.

But, you were at the beginning of a new era and the country was planning for the future and the future was to turn the old 'social order' upside down. In 1945, the standard rate of income tax was more than 40%, a higher rate was charged on incomes over £2,000 and saving was encouraged. The PAYE system ('pay as you earn') had been operating since 1944 and taxes were now deducted from wages by employers each week or month rather than being collected annually or twice yearly. Clothes were rationed but when not 'making do and mend', the government had intervened in the mass manufacture of high street fashions and 'utility' clothing could be bought free of purchase tax.

Newsprint was severely rationed but the popular papers, the **News of the World**, **The People**, the **Daily Express** and **The Daily Mirror**, reached most of the British homes, shaping public perceptions in the aftermath of the war.

Accommodation in cities was often scarce, unscrupulous landlords raised rents, but agricultural workers were provided with Government cottages. Cheap 'utility' furniture was still made; central heating was unheard of, coal fires heated houses – and coal was rationed. Children helped with the harvest; cinemas thrived for entertainment and newsreels and by 1945 although many pubs had closed due to enemy action, 'the local' was still a comforting place to go to - and everybody seemed to smoke!

WAR TIME BASIC RATIONS

On *average*, one adult

Bacon and ham - 4oz
1s 10d worth of meat - about 8oz
2oz butter
2oz cheese
4oz margarine
3 pts of milk
8oz of sugar
2oz tea leaves
1 Egg

POPULAR CULTURE

The "Top Ten" did not exist in 1945 but in America, the **Billboard Magazine** collected information on sales and radio 'plays' and gave us a "hit parade" of sorts. Many of the American artists, including, **Bing Crosby, Perry Como, The Andrew Sisters** and **Dick Haymes** were also very popular in Britain and their songs were heard on the radio and in the dance halls. At home, Vera Lynn remained 'the Forces sweetheart' and her iconic songs of the war years, **There'll Be Blue Birds Over** and

Vera Lynn sings to the troops.

A Nightingale Sang in Berkeley Square were still favourites. **Variety Bandbox** became a mainstay of the BBC Light Programme on Sunday evenings, featuring a mix of music and comedy, it launched or cemented the careers of many British performers including Dorothy Squires whose song, **The Gypsy** came out this year, whilst musical theatre and musical films produced many of the country's most popular songs too. **Sigh No More** was Noël Coward's first post war musical revue and the best-known song in the show, the wistful **Matelot**.

Magazines like **Picture Post, Punch, Women's Weekly, The Listener**, and many more, were relatively inexpensive and catered for most tastes. George Orwell's allegorical novella, **Animal Farm** was first published, as was Nancy Mitford's **The Pursuit of Love** and Evelyn Waugh's **Brideshead Revisited.**

In June, the opera **Peter Grimes** by Benjamin Britten, set in a fictional small town that bears a close resemblance to Britten's home of Aldeburgh, Suffolk, was performed for the first time at Sadler's Wells Theatre. Peter Pears, Britten's personal and professional partner, sang the title role.

WAR TIME SPORT

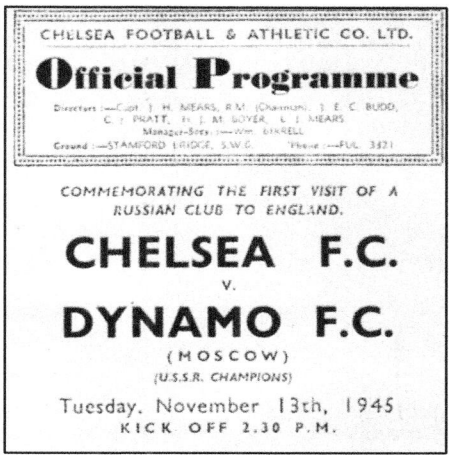

The war had finally ended and in a spirit of camaraderie, a Russian football team had been invited to tour Britain. They sent a club barely anyone in Britain knew: the league champions of the Soviet Union. Dynamo's first match was at a packed Stamford Bridge where after fast and furious football, the final whistle sounded for a 3-3 draw with Chelsea and the British crowd roared their approval for the Russians. By the end of the tour, British football fans would be wondering if they *were* the world's finest footballing nation and George Orwell was to refer to the tour as simply being *"war minus the shooting"*.

1950 THE YEAR

Education between the ages of 5 and 15 was made compulsory in 1944. In 1950, there were no state pre-schools or nurseries and all children who had now returned to their family having been evacuated from the towns and cities for the duration of the war, together with children who had stayed at home, would be setting off for school for the first time. It could be a very tearful day for both mother and child! But for the child, school life had a routine – calling the register, lessons, playtime and at mid-morning, a third-of-a-pint bottle of milk.

Reading, writing and arithmetic were most important; times tables were learnt by rote as was poetry; neat handwriting was practiced daily, and nature study was 'science' when leaves and acorns were identified and then later becoming 'arts and crafts'.

CHILDREN AT FIVE

Post-war rationing of sweets had finished in April 1949 and the jars on the shelves filled with blackjacks, barley sugar twists, sherbet Dabs, dolly mixture or toffees. Long queues formed outside sweet shops as children and adults engaged in a national 'sugar rush', meaning that four months later, rationing was reintroduced because of the sudden and unsustainable demand for sugar.

When going 'out to play', girls loved skipping or hopscotch whilst baby dolls slept in their prams and boys would generally rush around, play football, 'cops and robbers' or 'cowboys and Indians'.

HOW MUCH DID IT COST?

The Average Pay:	£464 (£9 p.w)
The Average House:	£1,900
Loaf of White Bread:	5½d (2p)
Pint of Milk:	5d (2p)
Pint of Beer:	1s 4d (7p)
Gallon of Petrol:	3s (3p per litre)
12mths Road Tax	£10
Newspapers:	1d - 3d (1p)
To post a letter in UK:	2½d (1p)
TV Licence B/White	£2 + £1 for a radio

POPULAR CULTURE

Music started to develop in 1950 making the UK a leading centre of popular music in the modern world. Brass and silver bands, music hall and dance bands, along with folk music, were starting to be replaced with American forms of music including swing and jazz. Nat King Cole had a huge hit with **Mona Lisa,** Frank Sinatra crooned **Goodnight Irene** but Billy Cotton was still going strong with his 'Wakey-Wake-aaaay!', followed by the band's signature tune **Somebody Stole My Gal.**

Jazz musician John Dankworth forms the **Dankworth Seven** and **Gracie Fields'** radio show transfers from the BBC to Radio Luxembourg.

Benjamin Britten's **Spring Symphony** premières at the Royal Albert Hall, London, and Herbert Howells' **Hymnus Paradisi** is also heard for the first time. New classical music includes Malcolm Arnold – **English Dances** for orchestra, and Britten's, **Lachrymae.**

The vibrant Opera scene includes Hugo Cole, **Asses' Ears**; Norman Demuth, **The Corn King**; Berthold Goldschmidt, Beatrice Cenci and Elisabeth Lutyens, **Penelope**.

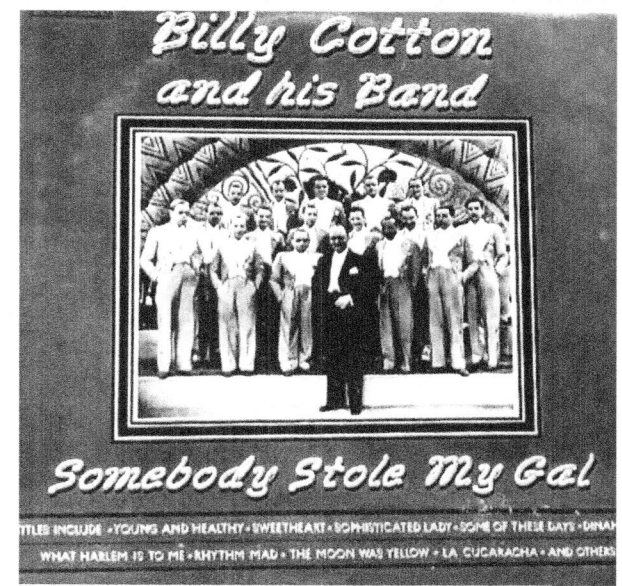

Musical theatre still held its allure and featured Noël Coward's, **Ace of Clubs**, Harry Parr Davies, **Dear Miss Phoebe** and Sandy Wilson's, **Caprice**

Going to the cinema was a cherished pastime, offering an escape into the world of romance, glamour and adventure. Musical films included, **Come Dance with Me**, featuring Anne Shelton, **Dance Hall**, starring Petula Clark and Diana Dors and **The Dancing Years**, starring Dennis Price.

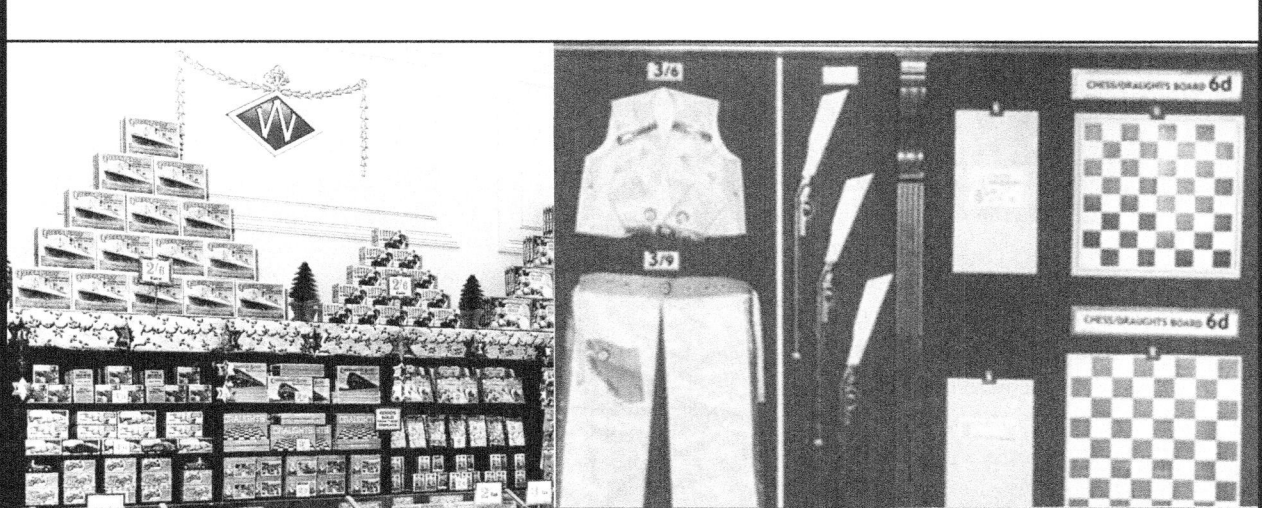

Woolworths was the shop for toys in 1950. During the war toys had been almost unattainable, but now, a limited range was back on the shelves. Cardboard Jigsaw Puzzles, Skittles, Carpentry Sets and Cowboys and Indians sets, all tempted the new generation.

How Life Was Changing

By 1956 austerity was beginning to end, unemployment was low and living standards were rising rapidly. The drab 'utility' styles from wartime were disappearing and colour was coming back.

The Clean Air Act was introduced to prevent pollution from smoke; Britain's first nuclear power station at Windscale was opened; the Karl Marx memorial is unveiled at a new grave site in Highgate Cemetery; Burgess & Maclean, two of the Cambridge spies, turn up in Moscow; British troops are under fire in the Suez Canal zone and Slough gets the UK's first double yellow lines.

Windscale Nuclear Power Station

Winning The Pools

Football Pools were a 'betting pool' for predicting the outcome of top-level football matches taking place in the coming week. It was typically cheap to play and entries were sent to Littlewoods or Vernons by post or collected from your home by agents. The most popular game was Treble Chance where you had to predict the matches to end in a draw.

Eleven In 1956

Age eleven was a milestone year for children. They went from being the 'king-pins' at primary school to 'the newcomers', either at Grammar School if they'd passed the 11+ exam or Secondary Modern if not. It was the start of growing up and independence but there was still plenty of fun to be had at home. Towns still had areas devastated by bomb damage providing excellent dens; parks had trees to climb; in the country, there were woods to explore, streams to paddle in or fish for 'sticklebacks' and those with bikes would cycle for miles on 'traffic free' roads.

How Much Did It Cost?

The Average Pay:	£580 (£10 18s p.w)
The Average House:	£2.000
Loaf of White Bread:	10½d (4p)
Pint of Milk:	7d (3p)
Pint of Beer:	2s (10p)
12mnths Road Tax	£12 10s
Gallon of Petrol:	5s 4d (5p/litre)
Newspapers:	2d - 5d (1-3p)
To post a letter in UK:	2½d (1p)
TV Licence	£3 b/white + £1 Radio

YOU WERE ELEVEN

POPULAR CULTURE

Elvis Presley has his first big hit in the UK with **Heartbreak Hotel** and Doris Day has a best-selling single with **Que Sera, Sera (whatever will be, will be.)** In Britain, the 2i's Coffee Bar opens in a basement in Old Compton Street, Soho, and it rapidly becomes a pioneering venue for rock & roll music. Tommy Steele was resident from July.

The first ever Eurovision Song Contest is held in Lugano, Switzerland. Only seven countries take part and Switzerland is the winner with **Refrain** sung by Lys Assia.

'Angry Young Man', John Osborne has the first performance of his play **Look Back in Anger** performed at the Royal Court Theatre. Alan Bates stars in his first major theatre role.

The hovercraft, an Air Cushion Vehicle, was invented by Briton, Christopher Cockerell. Aware of the Normandy landings in 1944, he wanted to find a way to transport troops safely up a beach, ideally at speed.

Rodgers and Hammerstein's musical, **The King and I** is released as a film starring Deborah Kerr and Yul Brynner. It is a huge success and nominated for nine Oscars, winning five whilst the wartime film, **Reach for the Sky** starring Kenneth More as Douglas Bader, wins the BAFTA Best British Film award.

Dodie Smith publishes her children's novel, **The Hundred and One Dalmations** and Gerald Durrell, his memoir, **My Family and Other** Animals; PG Tips introduce the **Chimpanzee's Tea Party**; Mettoy introduce **Corgi Toys** model cars; in Bristol, the first Berni Inn steakhouse opens and the new **Routemaster** bus forms part of the Lord Mayor's Show procession.

1960 The Year

In 1960, Harold Macmillan was presiding over a country which had a sense of community and life, and which after the war, was getting better astonishingly quickly. Towns and cities were being reshaped by a massive building programme of council estates, tower blocks and shopping centres.

Nigeria gained its independence from the UK; The Grand National was televised for the first time; 60,000 protestors staged a demonstration in London against nuclear weapons; Daimler Company was purchased by Jaguar Cars; Britain's first nuclear submarine HMS Dreadnought was launched by the Queen; black plastic bin bags were introduced for waste collection; the first episode of Coronation Street was aired on ITV and 31st Dec was the last day on which the farthing was legal tender.

New towns had tower blocks of flats and pedestrianised shopping centres with open spaces.

Penguin Books were found not guilty of obscenity in the Lady Chatterley's Lover case and the book sells 200,000 copies on the day the ban was lifted.

Life At Fifteen

Fifteen in 1960, you were now old enough to leave school and venture into the world of work, but not the armed forces; you still had to wait a year to legally buy cigarettes – and smoke them, and you couldn't buy a beer in a pub. The consumer boom had arrived with 'teen' clothes becoming available and fashion was influenced by America. Rock 'n' roll and film stars set fashions. There were the Teddy Boys and Beatniks.

How Much Did It Cost?

The Average Pay:	£700 (£13 p.w)
The Average House:	£2.235
Loaf of White Bread:	1s 2d (7p)
Pint of Milk:	8d (3p)
Pint of Beer:	1s 9d (9p)
Gallon of Petrol:	4s 8d (5p/litre)
12mnths Road Tax	£12 10s (£12.50)
Newspapers:	2d - 5d (1p - 2p)
To post a letter in UK:	3d (1p)
TV Licence	£4 Black & White

YOU WERE 15

POPULAR MUSIC

What Do You Want to Make Those Eyes at Me For? by Emile Ford & The Checkmates remained at number one from 1959. The first new number one of 1960 was **Starry Eyed** by Michael Holliday. **Little White Bull** by Tommy Steele, **Rawhide** by Frankie Laine, **Seven Little Girls Sitting in the Backseat** by The Avons and **Staccato's Theme** by Elmer Bernstein, reached their peak in 1960. Billy Fury, The Drifters, Ken Dodd, Roy Orbison and Sam Cooke all achieved their first UK chart top 10 single.

JANUARY **Jingle Bell Rock** by Max Bygraves reaches its peak at number seven and has had significant airplay every Christmas since.

MARCH **Poor Me** by Adam Faith was originally rejected by several music publishers as the original "Poor Man". It was felt by some that its style was like that of Buddy Holly.

APRIL **My Old Man's a Dustman** by Lonnie Donegan stayed at number one for four weeks.

MAY **Cathy's Clown** by The Everly Brothers was number one, telling the story of a man who was wronged and publicly humiliated by his lover.

LITTLE WHITE BULL
By MICHAEL PRATT, LIONEL BART and JIMMY BENNETT

TOMMY STEELE

ELVIS PRESLEY
IT'S NOW OR NEVER
MAKE ME KNOW IT

JUNE **Three Steps to Heaven** by Eddie Cochran made number one following his death in a car accident in April.

OCTOBER **Only the Lonely** was the first hit song for Roy Orbison.

NOVEMBER **It's Now or Never** by Elvis Presley was one of his bestselling singles and one of the best-selling physical singles of all time.

DECEMBER **I Love You** by Cliff Richard and The Shadows reached the Christmas number one.

Doctors and scientists were beginning to gather evidence that smoking could be harmful to your health, but in 1960 it was still promoted as a 'healthy', 'social' and 'fun' activity.

1966 THE YEAR

In 1966 Britain Harold Wilson was presiding over a country where the first 'baby boomers' were due to come of age and were intent on personal freedom and permissiveness. England won the World Cup for the first (and only) time; at the South Wales village of Aberfan a coal spoil tip collapses killing 144 (including 116 children); fridges, washing machines, cars and televisions were starting to become increasingly common place in households; London was officially declared "The Swinging City" in a Time Magazine cover story; The Severn Bridge was opened linking England to South Wales on the M4. Action Man, the toy figure, launched in the UK; John Lennon of The Beatles comments in an interview for the Evening Standard, "*We're more popular than Jesus now*" and Chi-Chi, the giant panda from London Zoo is flown to Moscow Zoo to meet with An-An.

THE WORLD CUP

1966 was the eighth FIFA World Cup, a national team men's senior football tournament held every four years. The tournament was played between the 11th and 30th July at Wembley stadium. England defeated West Germany 4–2 in the final to win their first ever World Cup title. The score was level 2–2 after 90 minutes and the match went to extra time. Geoff Hurst scored two goals to complete his hat-trick, the first to be scored in a men's World Cup final.

HOW MUCH DID IT COST?

The Average Pay:	£1,000 (£20 p.w)
The Average House:	£3,558
Loaf of White Bread:	1s 2½d (7p)
Pint of Milk:	9½d (4p)
Pint of Beer:	2s 6d (12.5p)
Gallon of Petrol:	5s 5d (6p per litre)
12mnths Road Tax	£17 10s
Newspapers:	4d - 9d (2p - 3p)
To post a letter in UK:	4d (2p)
TV Licence	£5 Black & White

POPULAR MUSIC & RADIO

The best-selling single in 1966 and the 10th biggest selling song of the 1960's was **Green, Green Grass of Home** by Tom Jones. The hit spent seven weeks at number-one and thirteen weeks in the top 10. The Spencer Davis Group and The Beatles had the joint most number one singles hits.

JANUARY - **Day Tripper/We Can Work It Out** by The Beatles, remained at number one for the first three weeks of 1966.

FEBRUARY - The first new number-one single of the year was **Keep on Running** by The Spencer Davis Group. **These Boots Are Made for Walkin'** by Nancy Sinatra made number one in February.

MARCH - **The Sun Ain't Gonna Shine Anymore** by The Walker Brothers got to number one.

APRIL – Another number-one hit for The Spencer Davis Group with **Somebody Help Me** was followed by **You Don't Have to Say You Love Me** by Dusty Springfield.

JUNE - **Paint It Black** by The Rolling Stones , with lyrics of grief and loss, and **Strangers in the Night** by Frank Sinatra were both number-one.

AUGUST – Number one, **Yellow Submarine/Eleanor Rigby** by The Beatles

SEPTEMBER - Jim Reeves, two years after he was killed in a plane crash, achieved his only UK number one single posthumously with **Distant Drums**, which spent five weeks at the top spot.

NOVEMBER - The Beach Boys, had four consecutive top 3 entries in the UK charts, **Good Vibrations**, reached number one for two weeks this month.

DECEMBER - The Christmas number-one hit in 1966 was **Green, Green Grass of Home** by Tom Jones.

The pirate stations **Swinging Radio** and **Britain Radio** launched in England in 1966.
Listen to This Space on the BBC Home Service made its debut along with **The Embassy Lark** on the Light Programme whilst **The Dales** and **Housewives Choice** continued to bring in listeners. In September, Terry Wogan made his debut on the BBC, presenting the Tuesday edition of **Late Night Extra** – "down the line" from Dublin.

January

28th The German army attempts to make their final advance but are defeated at the Battle of Bulge. From here onwards the Nazis are in full retreat.

February

13th The bombing of the German city of Dresden begins. Thousands of civilian lives will be lost over the next three days in air raids by over 1,300 Allied bombers.

March

7th British and American troops cross the Rhine for the first time.

29th The last bomb of the war is dropped on Britain; a German V1 rocket.

April 25th Russian and American troops meet at Torgau in Germany.

30th With Russian forces less than 500 metres from his Führerbunker, Adolf Hitler commits suicide.

May

2nd Berlin surrenders to the Russian army.

4th The German VII Army surrenders.

8th Victory in Europe is celebrated by crowds taking to the streets all across Allied Europe, America and the Empire. The day has since been celebrated as VE Day all over the world.

11th German forces in Czechoslovakia surrender.

An arranged photo commemorating the meeting of the Soviet and American armies, 2nd Lt. William Robertson (U.S. Army) and Lt. Alexander Silvashko (Red Army) stand facing one another with hands clasped.

April

13th Russian forces enter and capture Vienna.

18th 370,000 German prisoners are taken after the surrender of the Ruhr. All resistance in the area ceases.

Summary

On May 8, 1945, World War II in Europe came to an end. As the news of Germany's surrender reached the rest of the world, joyous crowds gathered to celebrate in the streets, clutching newspapers that declared Victory in Europe.

ENDED IN EUROPE

Field Marshal Wilhelm Keitel signing the unconditional surrender of the German Wehrmacht at the Soviet headquarters in Karlshorst, Berlin.

UNCONDITIONAL SURRENDER

Six years of war on a scale hitherto undreamt of was brought to a conclusion with the unconditional surrender of German forces on the 8th May 1945. Now known as *Victory in Europe Day,* the news of the Nazi defeat is still celebrated just as vigorously as it was at the time. Although the outpouring of joy in 1945 represented years of apprehension, fear and suffering, the majority of the British people had been expecting such an announcement since the end of 1944. Plans of 'post-war' Britain had already been put in place, and yet the day still brought mixed emotions for many; aside from the obvious celebrations, people mourned their loved ones as the day came to honour all those who had died in the fighting. It was also important to remember the large contingent of Allied troops still fighting the Japanese in the Pacific. In a speech on national radio, Prime Minister Winston Churchill said, '*We may allow ourselves a brief period of rejoicing; but let us not forget for a moment the toil and efforts that lie ahead';* a sober foreshadowing of the hardship that was still to come.

Adolf Hitler committed suicide on the 30th April, over a week before the final German surrender. In his place, Grand Admiral Karl Donitz did his best to negotiate terms for the end of the war, desperately attempting to make sure that as few Germans fell into the hands of the Russians as possible. As a result, Nazi occupied Denmark, Holland and Northwest Germany surrendered to Field Marshall Montgomery on the 4th May, followed by the unconditional surrender of all German forces to Allied Commander General Eisenhower on the 7th May; a further document was signed on the 8th in Berlin, thus successfully escaping thousands of Germans from inevitable Russian occupation.

January

19th The Burma Road is reopened.

February

19th US forces land on Iwo Jima, a Japanese island in Operation Detachment. The amphibious invasion comes after months of naval and ariel bombardment. Nearly 7,000 US Marines and over 30,000 Japanese soldiers died in this battle alone.

March

21st British forces regain control of Mandalay in Burma.

May

26th 700,000 incendiary bombs fall on Tokyo as US air raids drop over two thousand tons of explosives on the city in a bid to force a surrender. Over the space of two days, the majority of the city was left in ruins with the destruction of over 16 square miles. Somewhere between 80,000 and 100,000 civilians were killed. The Tokyo raid is the first of further campaigns on another 64 Japanese cities.

June

1st US troops land for the first time on Okinawa. The battle was one of the bloodiest of the whole war, with 14,000 US troops, and 70,000 Japanese soldiers killed. Over one third of the island's entire civilian population, some 150,000 people, were killed in the cross-fire. The US policy of 'island hopping' proved to be too costly for the American government and people, and influenced the decision to use nuclear weapons.

20th Australian troops land in Sarawak.

21st Okinawa is captured by US forces.

July

5th The Philippines is successfully liberated.

14th The Japanese cities of Honshu and Hokkaido are bombarded by the US Navy.

August

3rd Blockade of the Japanese home islands.

6th The world's first atomic bomb was dropped by the US on the Japanese city of Hiroshima. Between 60,000 and 80,000 people are killed instantly, with thousands of other injured. Approximately 67% of all structures in the city were obliterated. The US give Japan an ultimatum, suing for unconditional surrender.

8th Russia declares war on Japan.

9th The second US atomic bomb is dropped on the Japanese city of Nagasaki. Approximately 40,000 people are killed instantly. The second bomb had a 40% larger explosion yield than the first.

12th Soviet troops enter Korea.

14th Japan agrees to Allied surrender terms.

15th Victory in Japan Day.

SUMMARY

Japanese forces were in steady retreat across Burma, Malaysia and the Pacific Islands. They vowed never to surrender and the Allies knew that an invasion of Japan would be difficult and bloody. The use of atomic bombs in Hiroshima and Nagasaki and the Russian declaration of war against Japan forced an immediate surrender.

The signing of the Japanese Instrument of Surrender aboard the USS Missouri.

UNCONDITIONAL SURRENDER

It was in July, at the Potsdam Conference, the site where the conditions for the end of the European War were agreed, that there was the first offering for peace in the Pacific arena. Prime Minister Winston Churchill, President Truman and the President of the Republic of China Chiang Kai-shek issued the Potsdam Declaration, outlining terms for the Japanese surrender; these terms were promptly rejected, and it wasn't until the second atomic bomb was dropped by the US on the city of Nagasaki, that the Japanese finally surrendered. In a radio address to the Japanese public, Emperor Hirohito agreed to the Potsdam terms of complete surrender, disarmament, and the occupation of Japanese territory by Allied forces.

Celebrations across Britain and the United States hailed the true end to the Second World War, with President Truman describing the *Victory in Japan Day* as "*the day we have been waiting for since Pearl Harbour.*" A two-day holiday was announced in Britain and across the Empire, amidst a period of distinct change, with new British Prime Minister Clement Attlee delivering the news that "*the last of our enemies is laid low*" over British national radio. This was later backed up by the familiar voice of King George VI, who addressed the nation from Buckingham Palace with a celebratory yet sombre tone. "*Our hearts are full to overflowing, as are your own. Yet there is not one of us who has experienced this terrible war who does not realise that we shall feel it's inevitable consequences long after we have all forgotten our rejoicings today.*"

Official Japanese Allied occupation began on the 2nd of September, when 13,000 US troops entered Tokyo Bay aboard a convoy of over 40 ships. The Instrument of Surrender was signed by the Japanese foreign secretary on behalf of the Emperor.

Fountain Pen Fuse

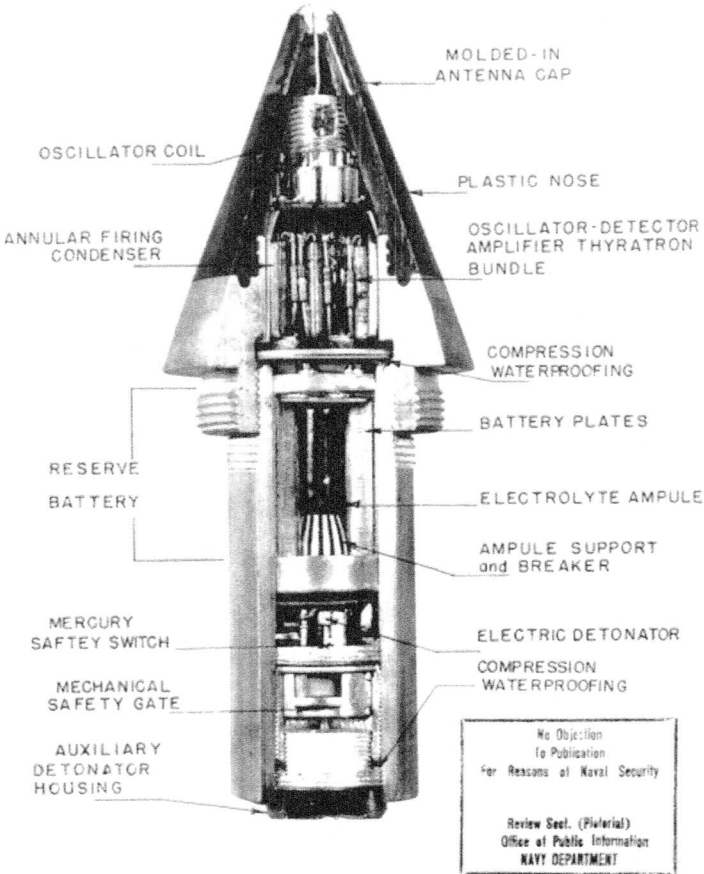

MOLDED-IN ANTENNA CAP

OSCILLATOR COIL

PLASTIC NOSE

ANNULAR FIRING CONDENSER

OSCILLATOR-DETECTOR AMPLIFIER THYRATRON BUNDLE

COMPRESSION WATERPROOFING

BATTERY PLATES

RESERVE BATTERY

ELECTROLYTE AMPULE

AMPULE SUPPORT and BREAKER

MERCURY SAFTEY SWITCH

ELECTRIC DETONATOR

COMPRESSION WATERPROOFING

MECHANICAL SAFETY GATE

AUXILIARY DETONATOR HOUSING

No Objection to Publication For Reasons of Naval Security

Review Sect. (Pictorial) Office of Public Information NAVY DEPARTMENT

Deemed to be one of the most potent weapons produced during the war, this projectile pen was revolutionary due to its delayed action fuse, known as the *L-Delay*. The fuse, similar in both size and shape to a regular fountain pen, contains a small piece of metal and a striker, separated by a spring, with the time of the fuse depending on how long it takes for the metal to snap once stretched by the spring. It was vital that the metal was of the same consistency throughout, and that the size of the grains that made the tip of the metal did not vary.

The metal, which is a lead alloy, is $7/10^{th}$ of an inch long and $3/16^{th}$ of an inch in diameter; in the middle is a neck and it is this neck that breaks and which had to be ground precisely to $1/10,000^{th}$ of an inch and, after hundreds of trials, the device became exceptionally accurate. The fuse could be scheduled to go off at times ranging from one hour to one month, as long as regular temperature was maintained and as a result, the explosive was used on every front from 1941 onwards.

The Foxer, the Hedgehog and the Sono

Details of Allied countermeasures against the fleet of German U-Boats have been revealed by Naval strategists, with intricate plans and designs culminating in the successful suppression of the German stealth submarines. Devices that enabled aircraft to listen to submarine movements underwater, confuse the targeting systems of U-Boat torpedoes, and mortars that fired multiple depth charges ahead of escort ships are just some of these measures that became so effective.

Not a single Allied ship that towed a *Foxer,* a device omitting sound astern of a vessel, was sunk by U-Boat torpedoes; the *Sono buoy,* a device dropped underwater containing a radio set allowing Allied forces to listen to submarine movements underwater disabled U-Boat's stealth capabilities; The *Hedgehog Mortar,* capable of throwing 24 projectiles over 200 yards ahead of a ship proved to confuse the U-Boat targeting systems.

Decoy Towns

Large decoy fires resembling a town in flames, decoy lighting and dummy airfields were amongst some of Britain's chief defences against German air raids during the war. The schemes, kept a close secret for the duration of the war in Europe, proved to be immensely successful, especially throughout the Battle of Britain and the Blitz in 1940 and 1941. It was estimated that decoy fires lured away 5% of all bombs and mines dropped at night, saving the lives of potentially as many as 2,500 people, and a further 3,000 injuries, not to mention the protection of property and infrastructure.

These decoy towns had the code name *Starfish* and were made up of three different types of flammable material that simulated that of urban destruction. In Cardiff over 150 bombs were drawn away in one night alone by just one *Starfish* facility; in fact, across 730 recorded attacks on decoys, casualties were only inflicted in four. Alongside this, decoy airfields played their part in confusing enemy targeting, to such an extent that by the end of the war, 443 attacks had been made on decoy airstrips, against 434 on real ones.

Firefighters in the London Blitz

D-Day Deception

In the weeks leading up to the D-Day offensive, Allied Commander General Eisenhower was placed in command of Operation Overlord, and with that, the strategic deception operation designed to put the Germans off the scent of the true D-Day operation. Eisenhower used several tactics to purposefully mislead the Nazi commanders into thinking the offensive was going to be staged at the Pas de Calais, rather than the Normandy beaches. Not only did Eisenhower 'leak' fake information through double agents, including a wild suggestion of Norway being a key landing spot, but also organised practical deceptions. A 'ghost army' was sent to Calais with a fake Mulberry Harbour - the artificial ports constructed by the allies - in such a way that it diverted attention away from the Normandy beaches, and fraudulent radio transmissions were made.

Entertainment At Home

The radio had been the most important medium for the people to get information during the war but the BBC had also provided much needed enjoyment. In July 1945, the BBC Light programme was launched, concentrating on mainstream light music and entertainment and taking over from the BBC General Forces Programme. **Family Favourites** at Sunday lunchtimes was extremely popular, linking those at home with loved ones who were still away and popular comedy programmes such as **ITMA – It's That Man Again**, **Much Binding in the Marsh** and **The Will Hay Programme**, drew in millions of listeners.

Entertainment Outside Home

The cinema was the mass entertainment of wartime and continued to be so. Again, it had been important for disseminating information but was particularly popular for Hollywood escapism but there were many British films too, romantic dramas and musicals. **The Wicked Lady** with Margaret Lockwood and James Mason had one of the largest audiences of the day, Rex Harrison and Constance Cummings brought Noël Coward's stage play **Blithe Spirit** to life on film.

What We Were Eating

Food was still rationed and seasonal, home grown, food was the order of the day - if you could grow some of your own, so much the better. Newspapers printed recipes and gave advice on how to turn dried eggs imported from America into omelettes, cakes and Yorkshire puddings but dishes were simple and with so little meat available, the nation embraced Spam.

What We Were Dancing To

When the Americans came to Britain, they brought with them exciting new dances such as the Jitterbug and swing bands played in dance halls and even works canteens, giving people the chance to forget austerity and enjoy themselves. In January 1945, a Jitterbug Contest was held with, "Captain Thomas of the US army willing to present One Pound to the winning couple in addition to the Prize."

1945 THE END OF WAR - THE END OF A GOVERNMENT

After the jubilation of the two victories and the end of the hostilities, the future still seemed uncertain for the British public. The mines and barbed wire were removed from the beaches, there was no more blackout and the Home Guard, the face of British defiance against Nazi aggression, was stood down. But many things also stayed the same, the war weary nation still faced rationing and Mr Middleton, a radio and TV gardener, continued to urge the nation to *'Dig for dear life'* and to *'force rhubarb, plant potatoes and sow peas'*.

For all the euphoria, Britain was virtually bankrupt, massively in debt to the United States and austerity increased after VE Day, with bacon and lard rations being reduced a few weeks' later, and bread rations introduced in 1946. However, life was going to change and Labour was elected to power in the General Election with a landslide victory, gaining 239 seats, 48% of the popular vote and achieving a majority of 145 seats, thus allowing Attlee to be appointed prime minister. This was the first time that the Labour Party had won an outright majority in Parliament, and allowed Attlee to begin implementing the party's post-war reforms for the country including putting the Beveridge Report of 1942 into action, plans for a new national insurance scheme – the National Health Service – and the 1944 Butler Education Act, which guaranteed the introduction of secondary education for all children.

JANUARY 1ST – 7TH 1945

IN THE NEWS

Monday 1 — **"New Year, Same Churchill"** A new year marks another emphatic speech by the Prime Minister, who claims that 1945 will *'bring us victory in Europe.'* Churchill spoke with his usual overbearing optimism, amidst calls for patriotism and strength of spirit.

Tuesday 2 — **"Get Your Skates On"** For the first time this winter, London's skaters hit the frozen lakes in Hampstead and Wimbledon as temperatures remained below freezing.

Wednesday 3 — **"Nationalisation of the Mines"** The National Union of Mineworkers, in conjunction with the Labour Party, have unveiled their campaign for nationalising the industry, after reports that youths would *'rather go to prison than work in the mines'*.

Thursday 4 — **"Crystal Palace Competition"** A competition wherein members of the public will be invited to design buildings for the restoration of Crystal Palace as a *'a place for education, recreation and the promotion of industry, commerce, and art'* has been approved.

Friday 5 — **"London to Paris Sea Rail"** The Ministry of War Transport are designing a London to Paris sea-rail service for a select number of civilian passengers wishing to travel to France later this year; travellers have been warned that hotels will be unavailable, and arrangements should be made in advance.

Saturday 6 — **"Cotton Calamity"** The Minister of Labour and National Service has spoken of the additional 17,000 men needed to fill the *'serious'* labour shortage in the cotton industry, which is already operating at a lowered capacity.

Sunday 7 — **"Making a Meal of It"** The Minister for Education has urged that the improving of school canteen facilities be second only to repairing war damaged houses.

HERE IN BRITAIN

"Boomerang Competition"

Lord Brabazon, unveiled a model aircraft exhibition on Regent's Street. The first of its kind in Britain, the exhibition includes models from members of over 500 modelling clubs across the country. Many are capable of flight, propelled by miniature engines.

Lord Brabazon spoke of his desire for participants to turn their fascination to the idea of the 'boomerang', and expressed his preparedness to launch a competition for their making and throwing. Brabazon added that he considered himself a *'first class'* thrower.

AROUND THE WORLD

"The Best of British"

A group of British farming experts, having returned from touring the United States and Canada, have spoken of the praise given to the British by their American and Canadian allies. The commended *'toughness'* of the British was paired with an unexpected understanding of British farming systems, and the issues faced by wartime economic struggles.

They added that there was *'no comparison'* between the women working on the fields in America and the efficiency of the Women's Land Army in England, despite the massive scale of the North American farms.

THE LONGITUDE LECTURE

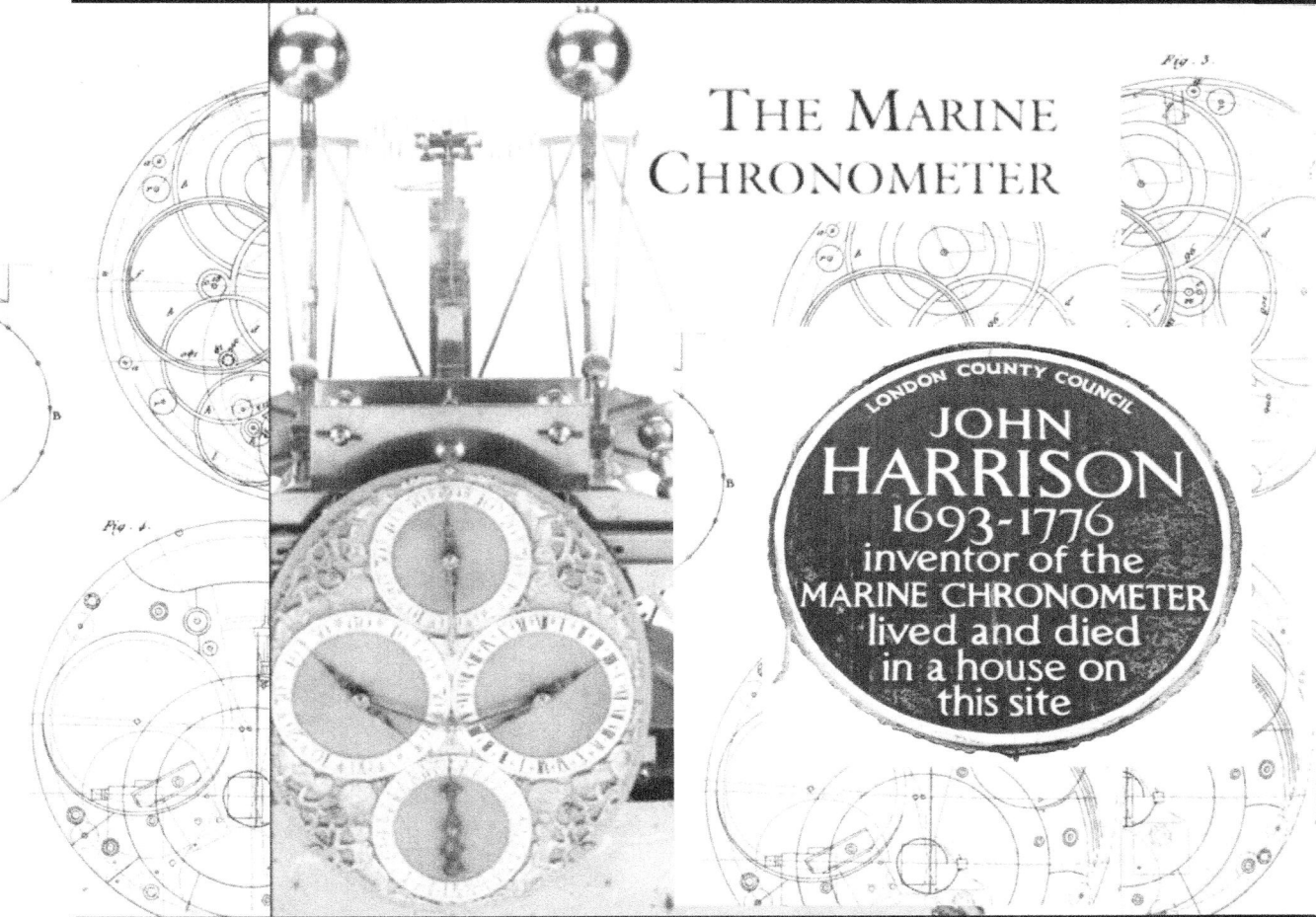

THE MARINE CHRONOMETER

LONDON COUNTY COUNCIL
JOHN HARRISON
1693-1776
inventor of the
MARINE CHRONOMETER
lived and died
in a house on
this site

Youthful anticipation filled the air of the Royal Institution this week, as the Astronomer Royal, Sir Harold Spencer Jones, gave a Christmas lecture to an audience of young astronomers. Spencer Jones informed on the discovery of longitude, commenting on the *'epoch making journey of Christopher Columbus'* and his struggles on his voyage home from the Bahamas knowing his Latitude but not his Longitude. This issue was faced by maritime travellers for hundreds of years and was considered well beyond the minds of those in Columbus' time. It wasn't until the middle of the 18th Century when the code was cracked with the invention of the Chronometer.

Spencer Jones also spoke of innovation from the period of Charles II and the establishment of the Institute in the first place. It was Charles II's idea to look to the stars as a means of determining longitudinal position; Charles' imperative of supporting the British Navy led him to establish a small committee, from which the first Astronomer Royal and the Institution was born. The first Astronomer Royal was set up with inadequate facilities, a salary of a measly £100 a year (£27,000 in today's money) and a *'silly, surly, labourer'* for assistance.

The Chronometer was born years later, with John Harrison's invention of a large clock-like instrument, winning him £20,000 prize money from the British Government. This, after subsequent, more accurate iterations, allowed sailors to navigate longitude with a genuine degree of accuracy, making it one of the most *'cherished possessions'* of the Institution. After the lecture, students were allowed to handle the 200 year old device.

JANUARY 8TH - 14TH 1945

IN THE NEWS

Monday 8   "**British War Oil**" Over 1,000 miles of oil pipelines have been hailed as a 'British achievement' by the government; the pipeline sees over 5 million tonnes of petroleum flow through it every day.

Tuesday 9   "**Now-Unforgotten Men**" Following news that the 14th Army in Burma have 'nicknamed' themselves 'The Forgotten Men,' there has been a call to ENSA for 'girls' to go out and entertain the troops in a hope that they might *bring an attitude of home'*.

Wednesday 10   "**The German Broadcasting Corporation**" A *'disparaging'* broadcast disguised as a BBC announcement has been confirmed as false by broadcasters as they spoke of the enemy's 'Arnhem Calling' supposed to erode the moral of the allied troops.

Thursday 11   "**Girls Get the Call Up**" All women born between 1920 and 1926 are to register with their local war office when they can, ahead of further labour shortages. Women have been told to prepare to take on vital domestic roles.

Friday 12   "**Air Ballot**" Postal voting has replaced the 'voting by proxy' system for men serving abroad ahead of the General Election this year. The Government announced the scheme for ballots to be transported by air from the continent.

Saturday 13   "**The Orchestra Played On**" There were no casualties when a V Bomb landed behind the stage at a pantomime in a Southbourne theatre. The orchestra continued to play, calming the audience.

Sunday 14   "**Last Week's Snow**" Parts of England experienced the heaviest snowfall of the winter with farmers in upland rural areas reporting drifts of up to 7ft. deep.

HERE IN BRITAIN

"The Guard's Chapel Gift"

After hearing about the tragic destruction of the Guard's Chapel in London by a flying bomb at the end of 1944, the 6th South African Armoured Division have donated £5,000 for its restoration.

This gift has been received with extreme gratitude from the War Office and with a note commending the *'unsurpassed courage and fighting qualities of his Majesty's Brigade of Guards.'* Although the money donated will cover the memorial's restoration, it is unlikely the project will be completed this year given the lack of facilities, resources and labour.

AROUND THE WORLD

"Anti-Blackout Flying Suits"

Hailed as one of the *'best kept secrets of the war,'* the US designed 'anti-blackout' flying suits are being worn by American fighter pilots to prevent them from passing out when coming out of a steep dive.

The extreme G forces felt by airmen during dog-fighting mean that the pressure exerted on them can be as much as seven times their body weight, putting immense strain on the body. The suit fits tightly around the pilot's lower body, where an automatic valve regulates pressure, preventing blood from draining to the legs.

The latest instalment of the Ministry of Information's popular information booklets sees the story of the Merchant Navy put forward in Epic format. The series, highlighting the heroics of various areas within the War Office and Armed Services, is exaggerated in typical propaganda fashion, to stir patriotism and interest in the war effort; a much-needed muster for enthusiasm after six long years of war. This particular story, tells of the trials and tribulations of merchant seamen throughout the war. Riddled with tales of heroics and beautiful illustrations, the Merchant Navy's edition of the public information leaflet maintains the high standard set by its predecessors.

It was one of the many duties of the Ministry of Information (MOI) to issue 'National Propaganda' to the masses, in order to inform and encourage involvement in the war effort. Amongst the many forms of media utilised by the MOI, the most successful became book-like leaflets that both informed and entertained in a largely exaggerated manner. Although the campaign began in disaster, with an internal dispute over copyright issues for documents, telegrams and reports, eventually, the first pamphlet 'Why Britain is at War,' became available for the public to purchase. Having been ridiculed by corporations such as W.H. Smith Ltd, who warned that 'nobody would want to buy it,' subsequent versions including 'The War at Sea' by 1940 had sold as many as 470,000 copies, been translated into three different languages and had been sold across Europe and the Middle East. 'The Battle of Britain' leaflet saw even greater success, selling over 2 million copies worldwide, over 300,000 of those coming in the first week. The implementation of dramatic images and illustrations proved to capture the imagination of people from all over the Empire.

IN THE NEWS

Monday 15   **"Paris Boat-Train"** The first civilian boat train since 1940 has left London for Paris, filled with representatives of firms to help the French reconstruction programme. Complete anonymity was maintained about leave location, ports and arrival stations.

Tuesday 16   **"Not Negotiable"** The Prime Minister was met with rapturous applause after declaring that the House would be unified against any suggestion of negotiation for peace with the axis powers, and that nothing other than complete surrender would suffice.

Wednesday 17   **"A Quick Trip to Australia"** A set of adapted Lancastrian bombers, able to hold nine passengers and capable of speeds up to 295mph are being trialled as the fastest civil aviation transport between England and Australia.

Thursday 18   **"Maple Tree for Friendship"** An infant Maple Tree, a gift to the nation from the mayor and people of Ottawa, was planted in Lincoln to mark the five-year anniversary of the establishment of the Royal Canadian Air Force there.

Friday 19   **"Ulsterman to the Rescue"** Amidst reports of severe labour shortages, the Prime Minister of Northern Ireland has pledged to send more labourers across the Irish Sea to aid in the reconstruction of London.

Saturday 20   **"Preventing Epidemics"** The United Nations Relief and Rehabilitation Administration (UNRRA) has signed an agreement on measures to prevent the spread of epidemics when mass repatriation of those exiled by the Nazi administration return to Germany.

Sunday 21   **"Girls to the Rescue"** the National Association of Training Corps for Girls aims to provide over 100,00 volunteers to help be a *'service to their community'.*

HERE IN BRITAIN

"Homes for Little Boys"

Field Marshall Montgomery has agreed to become President of the 'Homes for Little Boys' cottages in Kent. The Nineteenth Century houses are home to over 400 boys, half of whom are orphans.

Designed to create bright futures for underprivileged children, the boys cannot leave the cottages until they have completed either an apprenticeship in a chosen trade or joined the Armed Forces. In his acceptance speech, Montgomery emphasised the importance of *'good teamwork with others'* stating there is *'nothing you cannot achieve if you set your mind to it.'*

AROUND THE WORLD

"First to Four"

In his inaugural address as the first ever fourth term President of the United States, Mr Roosevelt spoke of his desire for *'lasting peace'*, not just in Europe but across the world.

In his long speech he thanked the American people for putting their trust in him once again, as he enters his 12th year as President, and called for steadfastness and continued strength in supporting the Allies on mainland Europe. Roosevelt's unprecedented success is no doubt aided by the trials and tribulations of war time command as the USA enters its 4th year of war.

WEALTH FROM WASTE

An exhibition organised by the Ministry of Supply has opened in London showcasing some of the imaginative and quirky items that have been recycled. Materials such as sawdust, oil and animal giblets are amongst those on display at the exhibition in their newly re-purposed forms; somewhat remarkably, residue blood from abattoirs is being used in the production of miner's helmets, giving an example for just how eccentric these ideas seem. Sawdust is already used in the production of phenolic plastics and resin board; it can be used as a fuel and has potentialities in the manufacture of industrial alcohol and of bricks and tiles. It has become a commonplace for waste oil to be filtered and re-used, and oily rags can be turned to good account in their yield of oil and of re-usable cloth. Companies are being encouraged to join one of the Ministry's salvage groups to work out how they too can reuse waste.

However, it is not just in industry where the re-purposing of waste product is proving vital; the Armed Forces are taking in hundreds of thousands of tonnes of animal fat and bones to be turned into explosive charges. Whilst a seemingly incomprehensible prospect, just a hundred tons of bones can be made into 12.5 tons of grease from which five tons of nitro-glycerine can be made, capable of providing the explosive charge for 40,000 18-pounder-shells. With each man producing, on average, 4lbs of fat and bones a day, the army's re-purposing scheme eclipses that of other industries. It's not only explosive shells that bones can help create, those same 100 tons of bones can also be reused as 12 tons of glue, or even 50 tons of pig food and fertiliser.

JANUARY 22ND - 28TH 1945

IN THE NEWS

Monday 22 — **"Sorbonne's Pomp and Pageantry"** General De Gaulle gave a speech at the reopening of the University of Sorbonne, commenting on the 'renaissance' of French intellectuals pioneering work on individual freedoms in an age of growing mechanisation.

Tuesday 23 — **"Gas Strike"** British Troops are being forced to man the Bradford Road Gas Works after the third strike in nine months disabled the plant. Under the advice of technical professionals, the men are experiencing a baptism of fire manning the ovens.

Wednesday 24 — **"Homes from the USA"** Over 30,000 temporary portable houses are being shipped from America to combat the housing crisis faced by bomb victims in Britain's major cities.

Thursday 25 — **"Potato Pause"** The extreme temperatures this winter has brought the planting and lifting of potatoes and sugar beet to a standstill. Instead, large crowds gathered around Lincolnshire farmland for tobogganing.

Friday 26 — **"ATS Girls Overseas"** Girls volunteering with the ATS are now *requesting* to be transferred overseas, contrary to the notion that the Government may need to invoke compulsory conscription.

Saturday 27 — **"Chemicals in the Water"** The Metropolitan Water Board have raised concerns over the *'unsatisfactory'* quality of the water passing through their filters as a result of factories expelling harmful chemicals into rivers and underground acquifers.

Sunday 28 — **"Naughty Girls Wouldn't Stand for It"** The *'Naughty Girls'* of Caernarvonshire have a strong dislike for policewomen and refuse to take orders from them,making this one of the only counties where women will not volunteer to be 'bobbies'.

HERE IN BRITAIN
"Heath Robinson"

A memorial exhibition dedicated to the recently deceased Heath Robinson has opened at the Fine Art Society. Robinson, famous for his drawings of elaborate designs and inventions differs greatly from the simplicity of the cartoonists of today and those in attendance at the exhibition may be amazed at the technical proficiency of the eccentric designs or wowed by the finesse and fluency of his drawings. Robinson's popularity on the cartoon circuit is evidenced by the exhibition containing many of his fan favourites including "Incriminating Evidence," and "An Easy Way to Make Your Own Hard Tennis Court."

AROUND THE WORLD

"Black Market Brussels"

Scotland Yard Detectives remain stumped in their investigation to uncover the black market of army equipment in Brussels. The extensive underground network has become not so underground in recent months, with sellers becoming bolder in their operations.

Customers are able to buy items like beef and cigarettes, but can even acquire Jeeps. So far, police have not been able to do much about the growing issue, given the restrictive Belgian laws stating that possession is a necessity for arrest; given this fact, suspicion or even advertisement of black-market goods is not an offence.

BURNS NIGHT

Piping in the haggis.
The INSET shows a portrait of Robbie Burns.

Robert Burns was born in Ayrshire on the west coast of Scotland in 1759, the eldest of 7 children. His birthday on 25th January, has been marked for over 200 years with feasting and recitations of his works among Scots and Hibernophiles all over the world. His father was a poor and relatively unsuccessful tenant farmer, and Robert's childhood was marked by poverty and hard manual work. Educated to read and write mainly by his self-taught father, he wrote many poems and songs in Scottish dialect while working as a farm labourer. It was only later on in life that his work about the themes of love and nature, was published and became very popular. Burns fathered twelve children to four different women, the last being born on the day he died, 21st July 1796.

Burns Night Suppers are held the world over, and in Scotland are more widely observed than that of its patron saint, St. Andrew, on 30th November. The suppers generally follow the same format with a welcome to the guests, and announcements, following which the 'Selkirk Grace' is recited. Then the haggis, the 'great chieftain o' the pudding-race' a traditional meat and herb pudding, is brought in on a silver tray, piped in by a bagpipe player. 'Address To a Haggis' is recited while the haggis is served with neeps and tatties, as potatoes and turnips are called, and drams of whisky. Afterwards many of his other poems will be recited and often there will be dancing. The evening finishes with the singing of the traditional song 'Auld Lang Syne' which Burns based on an older Scottish folk song. To this day it is traditionally sung to bid farewell to the old year at the stroke of midnight on Hogmanay (New Year's Eve).

JAN 29TH - FEB 4TH 1945

IN THE NEWS

Monday 29   **"A Welcome Like No Other"** The Duke and Duchess of Gloucester have been welcomed in triumphant fashion as they arrived in Sydney for their tour of Australia. Thousands lined the streets and the greeting was described as *'unparalleled.'*

Tuesday 30   **"The Great Thaw"** The great frost that gripped Britain over the last couple of weeks has given way to an even greater thaw, which began unexpectedly and rapidly. After heavy snowfall Monday night, the streets were filled with slush throughout the day.

Wednesday 31 **"New and Improved Austins"** Thirty new Austin cars are sitting in the showroom window for distributors and dealers to inspect at the company's factory in Birmingham. The new and improved engines in the cars are capable of up to 16 brake horse power.

Thursday Feb 1 **"No More Women War Correspondents"** The Empire Press Union is again discussing the disqualification of British female war correspondents, a policy which will be considered by the War Office. Women are permitted licenses only in Canada, Australia and America.

Friday 2   **"The Great Return"** 721 sick and wounded prisoners of war have arrived in Liverpool after making the trip from the continent by ship. The men will be given a thorough medical evaluation and 42 days paid leave.

Saturday 3   **"Perambulator Prices"** The Board of Trade has announced a maximum retail price for prams and pushchairs following the improved supply of materials for production. The target for the year is over 400,000 prams.

Sunday 4   **"A Woman's View"** Over 25,000 angry women have written to local councils and the Government over a refusal to accept a female input in the planning of post war houses.

HERE IN BRITAIN

"Airborne Operations"

In what appears to be a bid to disprove the allegations that the RAF were disbanding their glider regiment, the Air Ministry have announced a new programme in which airmen will take part in airborne operations in gliders. This is no mean feat, as gliders need a largely different skill set to powered aircraft, the project is being approached with enthusiasm by both the army and the air force alike.

The new glider squadrons will take the majority of their airmen from the already large pool of powered aircraft pilots and will be trained extensively in ground combat.

AROUND THE WORLD

"Stalingrad Anniversary"

On the second anniversary of the German defeat at Stalingrad, British and Soviet delegates met at the Soviet Embassy in London, when gifts were handed over to the British craftsmen who made the Sword of Honour presented by our King to Stalingrad.

They were albums bound in ribbed scarlet silk, with a gilt clasp, each containing a photographic record of life in Stalingrad before, during, and after the memorable siege and signed by citizens of the city, with greetings to the British, and reproductions of letters sent to Mr Stalin by Churchill and Roosevelt.

THE YMCA

A YMCA mobile catering van serving tea in North Africa in 1942 (Top Photo).

The photo BELOW shows the Ridgewood YMCA hut on the Western Front in 1917.

Established in 1844, the 'Young Men's Christian Association' began life as a prayer and Bible study group. Over the next century, it played a role in saving and supporting countless numbers of servicemen throughout two World Wars, donating millions of pounds to many causes and also becoming one of the most influential aspects of civilian support during the First World War. Activities included film showings, libraries, religious services, concert parties, folk dancing and educational lectures. £158m was spent on tea and other refreshments, a further £55m on relief stations both in England and France, and £7m on notepaper to accommodate the 200 million letters that were written home from the Continent. Many of the 40,000 volunteers working with the YMCA, especially those who lost their lives aiding servicemen in France, received civilian and military honours, and all were endowed with special recognition by the Commonwealth War Graves Association for their services.

The story during the Second World War is similar; their second-hand vans, painted camouflage green, were first used in East London and by the end of 1940 there were 500 vans bringing refreshments to troops, rescue workers and victims of bombing raids. Mobile canteens were in place in France right from the outbreak of the war and were present on the Dunkirk and Normandy beaches until the end. Throughout the war, the YMCA trailed the advancing and withdrawing Allied armies, where, as well as serving mugs of tea, they sold cigarettes, cake and essentials such as toothpaste. The huts of the First World War were static, but the tea car was mobile for increasingly changeable theatres of war. YMCA's world fellowship came into its own as the war progressed: tea cars, cinema vans, and mobile libraries bearing the red triangle of YMCA were a common sight.

FEBRUARY 5TH - 11TH 1945

IN THE NEWS

Monday 5   **"Colston Halls Burning"** Colston Hall, which housed some of Bristol's most iconic political and entertainment events, burnt down in the early hours of the morning, causing more than £200,000 worth of damage.

Tuesday 6   **"New Zealand Day"** The 105th Anniversary of New Zealand independence is being celebrated with a number of events across the country. The first Treaty of independence was signed by Queen Victoria in 1840.

Wednesday 7   **"Abolition of Domestic Drudgery"** The influence of the *'progressive views of a woman'* have been attributed to the implementation of new bright colours on items in the gas and kitchen planning exhibition.

Thursday 8   **"Bomb Alley Order"** A licence is now required to carry out any building work costing over £10 within a *'reasonable working distance to London'*, and for homes that are in urgent need of repair in and around so named 'Bomb Alley's' across the country.

Friday 9   **"Raising Lock Tummel"** Plans for a new hydro-electric project in the Scottish Highlands would involve raising the level of Loch Tummel by almost 17 feet through the construction of a damn. Fishing may suffer, even with a fish pass.

Saturday 10   **"Secret Lake"** An anonymous gift of over 140 acres of land including Boon Crag Farm and Monk Coniston Hall, has been donated to the National Trust. Some of the land will be leased to the Holiday Fellowship.

Sunday 11   **"Tired but Cheerful"** Over 500 Dutch children, mainly orphans, aged between 8 and 15 have arrived in London from where they will be sent to a number of hostels and wartime homes across the Midlands.

HERE IN BRITAIN

"End of Balloon Command"

Following the decrease in the need for air defence of British towns and cities, the RAF Balloon Command is being disbanded after eight years.

At the beginning of the war, the RAF had only 600 balloons in their armoury but by the Blitz this number was at over 2,400 and in London alone, the balloons are attributed to stopping almost 300 flying bombs over the last year.

The Air Minister gave his thanks to the division, paying homage to its service both at home and abroad - where the service will continue.

AROUND THE WORLD

"Tickets from the Sky"

To celebrate the birthday of King Farouk, the King of Egypt, fantastic celebrations were held throughout the country. Aircraft flew across towns dropping packets of sweets hung from miniature parachutes and free train tickets for the public to attend celebrations in the Capital where The King was greeted to cheers from thousands of visitors outside the Royal Palace. The main celebration was a 121-mile marathon carried out by a relay team of Egyptian soldiers, who broke the race down into legs, carrying a flaming torch between the Royal Palace in Alexandria and Cairo.

BALLET IN BRUSSELS

The famous Sadler Well's Ballet is in Brussels performing the second of their three week show at the Garrison Variety Theatre. Hundreds of servicemen and women, either on leave or stationed in Belgium, are flocking to the venue daily to see, what is for many, their first ballet. Unfortunately, not all the ballet's company could make the trip from London due to harshly imposed age restrictions associated with the risk of travel to the Continent, meaning that a few very talented young people are not able to showcase their talent on the European stage quite yet. Nevertheless, the imposition has hardly faltered the dancers, who have dazzled the Belgian capital with daily performances.

Although their first appearance in Belgium has been hailed a unanimous success, the journey to their shows was far from smooth. Their journey to Brussels was tediously delayed through gales in the Channel and they arrived, behind schedule, having expected to perform at Paris in the first instance. They came at a time of intense cold, and the troupe were hindered by gas leaks, heating problems, freezing temperatures and flooded auditoriums. When the issue of the coal supply, preventing the heating, was finally resolved, the soaking wet seats and floors erupted with plumes of evaporating smoke. Plus, the somewhat unexpected quantity of baggage which, including set props and costumes, weighed a total of 17 tons, meant that the company were unable to stop and perform at a forward station in Holland, meaning the duration of their stay would instead be spent in Brussels. These setbacks however, failed to dampen the English dancer's resolve, as the troupe remained in good spirits for the duration of the journey. The revised plan will see the performers pass back through Paris returning to England by March.

FEBRUARY 12TH - 18TH 1945

IN THE NEWS

Monday 12 "Victory Plans" The military plans preparing for the final defeat of Hitler have been drawn up by the *Big Three* at a military conference in Yalta. Churchill met with President Roosevelt and Marshal Stalin where they discussed the terms for no surrender.

Tuesday 13 "Women's Press Club of London" The Minister of Information was among guests at the opening of the first Women's Press Club of London. Formed from a meeting of women journalists in 1943, the organisation now boasts over 300 members.

Wednesday 14 "SSAFA 60th Birthday" The Soldiers', Sailors', and Airmen's Families Association celebrate their 60th Birthday having helped over 2 million families since the outbreak of the war. Founded in 1885, the organisation helps with personal aid for families of those serving.

Thursday 15 "No Allowance for First Child" The Government has proposed a new Family Allowance scheme in which parents are allocated 5s a week for each child *after* the first born.

Friday 16 "Paper Packs a Punch" An exhibition has opened in Birmingham to create awareness of the need for wastepaper. 2,000 tons a day is needed. It takes 15,000 tons of wastepaper each day to create enough wallboard to repair damage in London alone.

Saturday 17 "Ice Cream for Patients" Ice Cream machines are in the process of being installed in war hospitals across the country in the hope that it may be served as a *'general article of diet'* to recovering patients.

Sunday 18 "Washington Deeds" The deed of land transfer signed some 350 years ago, was presented to the owners of Sulgrave Manor, the historic home of George Washington. The deeds were inscribed with the Washington Coat of Arms.

HERE IN BRITAIN

"Lady D Resigns"

Lady Denman has resigned as the Honorary Director of the Women's Land Army saying, *'The Land Army is a uniformed service and the work which its members have undertaken, often at considerable financial sacrifice, is in my view as arduous and exacting as any branch of women's war work and of great national importance.*
Yet they have been refused post-war benefits and privileges accorded to such other uniformed and nationally organized services as the W.R.N.S., the A.T.S., the W.A.A.F., the Civil Nursing Reserve, the Police Auxiliaries, and the Civil Defence Services.'

AROUND THE WORLD

"Rescheduled World Jamboree 1941"

The rescheduled Boy Scout World Jamboree is set to be held in Paris in the summer of next year. Originally scheduled for 1941, the event will be the sixth of its kind and attended by over 20,000 Scouts from across Europe. It is believed that French infrastructure will be of a suitable level by 1946 to adequately transport the arriving boys.
The International Commissioner for the Scouting movement paid tribute to the enduring spirit of French Scouts, who did not cease their activities even under Nazi occupation throughout the past few years.

VALENTINE'S DAY

An influx of Valentine's Day cards and gifts have flooded the post this year, with people more inclined than ever to show affection to their loved ones by turning to the custom of romantic and charming Valentine's Day festivities on February 14th. British love makers have flocked to card and chocolate shops to buy gifts as the country gets swept up with the air of love.

The Valentine's Day festival itself is somewhat mysterious in origin, with multiple different sources offering multiple different views. The trail goes back to the Saint Valentine, or one of three possible Saint Valentines, all of whom were martyred. The most recognised saint of the three, defied the Roman Emperor Claudius after he outlawed marriage for young men, by continuing to perform marriage ceremonies for young lovers in the street. He was beheaded for his treason. Others suggest that Saint Valentine was a Bishop also beheaded by Claudius and the third, a Valentine killed for helping Christians escape the cruelty of Roman prisons. According to one legend, an imprisoned Valentine sent the first 'Valentine greeting' to a young girl he had fallen in love with, possibly his captor's daughter, and he signed his letter *'from your Valentine'*- an expression still used to this day.

The festival itself, nevertheless, acts as a celebration of the life of Saint Valentine, possibly all three Saint Valentines, but wasn't an overtly romantic celebration until characterised as such by Geoffrey Chaucer in his 1375 poem, *'For this was sent on Seynt Valentyne's day … whan every foul cometh ther to chese his make'*. The oldest known valentine was a poem written in 1415 by Charles, Duke of Orleans, to his wife while he was imprisoned in the Tower of London following his capture at the Battle of Agincourt.

IN THE NEWS

Monday 19   **"Country House"** The practice where candidates stay in a 'country house' to take a series of psychological tests, as used by the Armed Forces to appoint officers, is to be trialled by the Civil Service for the highest administrative positions.

Tuesday 20   **"Heath Row Airport"** No plans have yet been released for the re-purposing of airfields in and around London after the end of the war. Particular interest is on the partially built airfield, Heath Row, whose use as a military base now seems unlikely.

Wednesday 21 **"Cold Winter"** The end of 1945 may be a cold one for many, as the Regional Fuel Controller revealed that Britain has used almost all its coal reserves. It is suspected that the end of the war would accentuate, not reduce, this problem.

Thursday 22   **"Shortage of Yarn"** The Board of Trade has revealed its concern over a severe shortage of yarn, despite an excess of cotton in Britain. The necessary supply of warm clothes to the public whilst producing further war clothing, is exacerbating the situation.

Friday 23   **"Royal Biology Lesson"** The King and Queen sat for over 15 minutes in a dark room watching an X-Ray film explaining how the human body works. The Queen described the lecture as *'one of the most interesting films I have ever seen.'*

Saturday 24   **"The Boat Race"** Cambridge came through as the underdogs to beat Oxford in the fourth war-time Boat Race. Thousands saw it run on the Henley Royal Regatta course.

Sunday 25   **"Red Army Day"** Both the royal family and the Prime Minister have paid tribute to Marshal Stalin as Russia celebrates its 27th Red Army Day.

HERE IN BRITAIN

"Tinker, Tailor, Teacher, Spy"

An English teacher working in Paris has been charged with the intention to assist the enemy after he was caught supplying literature to the German War Office for use as propaganda. During the trial, Mr Hewitt expressed his guilt and offered to work on countermeasures to misinform German radio channels.

Nevertheless, the verdict marks the first British citizen to be found guilty of fraternising with the enemy throughout the whole war period. It was revealed that Hewitt was still accepting German payment until the end of 1944.

AROUND THE WORLD

"Red Army Day"

Red Army Day will be spent with most of the Russian forces posted abroad as the army pushes to just 60 miles outside Berlin. Troops are occupying areas that have not been invaded since the Middle Ages and the crimson red flag can be seen in the German military stronghold of Marienburg.

The success is being celebrated across Russia, especially in recently liberated areas that had been under German occupation. The fact that the successes coincide with the 27th anniversary of the Revolution makes the celebrations more emphatic.

THE ATLANTIC BRIDGE

NORTH ATLANTIC CROSSROADS

DARRELL HILLIER

FERRY COMMAND

On Armistice Day in 1940, the first of what turned out to be thousands of aircraft made the journey from Newfoundland to Scotland, marking the beginning of the now integral Air Ferry Service between America and Britain. When the seven Hudson bomber aircraft landed in Scotland, led by now Air Vice Marshal Bennet, it was a welcome addition to the much-needed reinforcements for the RAF, and that was only the beginning. The steady and continuous stream of American aircraft has proved invaluable for the Allies over the course of the last four years, and the route was accurately called, the 'Atlantic Ferry' service. The release of a book containing the full story of the trials and tribulations of the flights has been published, containing previously top-secret information only recently released by the Air Ministry.

What is now known as Transport Command, a branch of the Air Force, has gone through a number of name changes over its four years of operations; beginning life as the Atlantic Ferry Organisation, and subsequently being swallowed by the RAF and renamed Ferry Command, the shuttling of aircraft expanded from just between the US and the UK, to networks all across Europe and the Middle East throughout the Second World War. Aircraft supplied by the US armed forces would be flown to Scotland, given a quick RAF paint job, and then deployed to various allied airbases in England, France, the Middle East, the Mediterranean and even India. It is important not to understate the extent of this achievement; the passage between Canada and Scotland was treacherous, and months of planning had to be carried out in order to ensure safety for both aircraft and pilots. The hard work paid off however, as between 1940 and 1945, not a single aircraft was intercepted by the enemy.

FEB 26TH - MARCH 4TH 1945

IN THE NEWS

Monday 26   **"Industrial Makeover"** Wales has been named as the site for the development of the Board of Trade's new interest, nylon yarn. Work is scheduled to begin on a 2m sq ft factory; the industry would employ over 1700 people.

Tuesday 27   **"The Barrage Power Scheme"** The Barrage Power Scheme has been given the go ahead by the Minister of Fuel and Power. The construction of a hydro-electricity plant on the banks of the River Severn could begin as early as 1947 and be operational by 1955.

Wednesday 28 **"Back Bike Lights"** A letter by six cyclist organisations has objected to the new Bill mandating the fitting of rear lights on bicycles, stating that white reflector strips are just as, if not more, effective.

Thurs March 1 **"Too Good to be True"** remarked the Queen as she viewed a thermostat-controlled oven at the electric kitchen exhibition in London. Her majesty was left bewildered when shown the device, which contains a red light to indicate correct temperature.

Friday 2   **"Liverpool Living"** Over 90,000 new houses in the next 25 years are the parameters set by the Mayor of Liverpool. He was viewing a new proposed dwelling of a £500, narrow fronted, bungalow.

Saturday 3   **"Scottish Mining Strike"** Many mining pits across Scotland have been left idle or at limited capacity following the strike of over 7,000 workers across the country. Firemen have been brought in to help where possible.

Sunday 4   **"Staggered Holidays"** To help ease the burden on public transport in the holiday season, the Government has announced a new scheme to stagger holidays across the summer.

HERE IN BRITAIN

"Radio Silence"

A secret exhibition of radio technology developed especially for use in the Far East, has attracted attention from several Allied powers. Items demonstrate the *'tropicalisation'* of radio equipment for swamps, monsoons and jungle uses, including the range of miniature components designed with a view to economising weight so that complete apparatus can be transported easily by air or on the backs of pack mules, and pocket-watch sized loudspeakers. Wire used in some of the components is so fine as to be almost invisible to the naked eye.

AROUND THE WORLD

"Frogs and Fleas by Air"

Throughout the war, several strange items have been transported by British aircraft, serving even more bizarre purposes. Some of the most unique of these come in the form of animals, tested in the name of medical research. Live frogs have made numerous trips between England and South Africa with *'Water must be changed at Cairo'* inscribed on each box. Fleas from Sierra Leone and guinea pigs for the treatment of smallpox have proved invaluable for medical purposes and the success of the transportation of this various 'livestock' opens up possibilities for after the war.

A Soldier's Best Friend

The old adage that a dog is *man's best friend* is no truer than in the 14th Army in Burma, where soldiers keep pets in their hundreds. There is not a single dog in the Far East that will go hungry if the British Army are stationed there, with mutual agreements being struck between man and animal daily. In return for food and shelter, the men are getting companionship and dispensing pent-up paternal expression in ways that are the closest simulation of home many have felt since the beginning of the war. The wave sweeping across the British forces is no more pronounced than in the Far East, where General Li-Jen, commander of the first Chinese Army, has seven puppies in his ownership.

However, it is not just dogs that the men have taken to keeping, almost every animal, domestic or otherwise, has been tried. An officer in the Burma Intelligence Corps keeps a bear cub, which was unfortunately kicked out from the Hotel Calcutta for eating the end of a bed. An officer from the fifth Indian division successfully tamed a sheep, which now follows and patiently waits for its master during activities and a Sergeant is in possession of a 10-foot python, which is his pride and joy. Almost every unit has some form of poultry farm at its base and at least one somewhat unconventional pet amongst its ranks.

The story of the week, however, comes from a Derbyshire Corporal, who successfully oversaw the birth of several turkeys on the roadside, and he is protecting them to ensure they don't meet the fate of many of their ancestors. When asked, he revealed his plans to take the turkeys back with him to England, where they can live a happy life in the fields of Derbyshire!

IN THE NEWS

Monday 5   **"Dock Discipline"** 3,000 soldiers are taking on the work of 7,000 striking London dockers. The strike is over the creation of a new Board of Control which lacks worker representation.

Tuesday 6   **"Royal Transport"** The King has authorised the honorary rank of 'Second Subaltern for the Auxiliary Territorial Service' to the Princess Elizabeth who is 19 next month and has completed the first stage of her training with the ATS.

Wednesday 7   **"Royal Visit"** The King and Queen have travelled over 100 miles across the North visiting factories and locations that have played a key part in the war effort. The surprise visit included locations in Liverpool and Lancashire.

Thursday 8   **"Tug Masters"** At a celebratory dinner, the First Lord of the Admiralty toasted the 20 tug masters who led over two thousand ships that towed the Mulberry Harbours between England and France during the D-Day Landings and then afterwards, handled vital military cargoes totalling 2m tons of shipping.

Friday 9   **"The Allowances Bill"** During the second reading in Parliament for the Family Allowances Bill, members have been promised a 'free vote' on whether the money should be paid to the man or the woman in the household. The estimated cost is over £60 million.

Saturday 10   **"Britain's Farms Need You"** A plea has been sent out requesting help from over 200,000 men or women to help with the raising and harvesting of this season's crops.

Sunday 11   **"National Holiday Centre"** A 7,000 room, national holiday centre, has been proposed by the Sussex Town Planning Consultant in the hope of 'saving' his area of coastline. The financial situation of the county is becoming a concern for the council.

HERE IN BRITAIN

"The Sale Room"

A first Folio Shakespeare, published in 1683, has been sold at auction for £1,800. What was once sold for £1 and labelled as the *property of a lady,* the book attracted a lot of attention from collectors and enthusiasts alike.

The small example of one of the world's most famous books was not in a perfect condition and the portrait on the title appeared to be a copy. The book has at least 32 defects and was bound with fragments of an old cotton dress belonging to Lady Southey, the wife of the seller.

AROUND THE WORLD

"The Yellow Duck"

A letter sent to The Times newspaper by Sir Sydney Cockerell in December 1944 entitled, 'The Yellow Duck' is now the basis for a Swedish led appeal for toys to give to the disaffected children of liberated Europe.

The 'Yellow Duck' story describes the ecstasy of Greek children who had never before seen such a toy and has taken the country by storm, inspiring the 'Save the Children Fund' in Sweden. The plea for money and toys has been readily received by the public, with the first donation from the Crown Princess of Sweden.

THE ROYAL AIR FORCE

A WWI Sopwith (top left).
A WWII Spitfire (front right) and
Hurricane (rear right) and a Lancaster
bomber (front left).

Sir Archibald Sinclair has given a rousing speech to the House of Commons describing the achievements of the Royal Air Force throughout the war, including, but far from limited to, the foiling of the German counter-invasion, and the success of the combined Anglo-American offensive on the German oil reserves, which are now in dwindling supply. Although the German use of the V2 bombs has caused the destruction of homes across the South, the work of the RAF in conjunction with the army, has prevented larger scale destruction.

When the war of 1914 started, the aeroplane was a new and untried weapon, strictly limited in its uses and not sure of its role. Rapidly it developed both as a weapon of offence and defence. When the allies mounted their counter-offensive in 1918, the RAF was able to concentrate 1,290 first-line aircraft against its opponents' 340, and, enjoying this air superiority, was able to disrupt the Germans' communications and harass their troops by low flying attacks. When the WWI Armistice came, the RAF was the greatest air force in the world, possessing more than 200 squadrons, 22,647 aircraft of all, 103 airships and a total strength of 291,000 officers and men. After the war the Service shrank to a shadow of its former self but managed to keep many members possessing a pioneering spirit, which in turn, maintained the high standards and increased the prestige of British aviation throughout the world.

At the beginning of this war, we had far fewer planes than Germany and the country has undergone a massive drive to build Spitfires and Hurricane fighters, and Wellington, Whitley and Hampden bombers. All technically superior to the German planes, but it was, nonetheless, a dangerous situation until the Battle of Britain had been won.

MARCH 13TH - 18TH 1945

IN THE NEWS

Monday 12 — **"Penicillin Production"** The Ministry of Supply and Health has announced the rapid increase in the production of penicillin and that supplies will shortly reach over 200 hospitals across the country; there will soon be enough penicillin for all needs.

Tuesday 13 — **"Flying Boat"** Information surrounding plans for the largest ever civil aviation, flying boat has been released. The boat will be capable of transporting 50 – 100 passengers.

Wednesday 14 **"Tunnelling to Berlin"** 67 German prisoners of war, most of them officers, escaped a Prisoner of War Camp in Glamorgan. 40 have since been recaptured.

Thursday 15 — **"Around the Commonwealth in 52 Days"** Returning from Canada, Lord Reith concluded his 52-day long, 44,500-mile, tour of the Commonwealth as Head of the British Delegation on Commonwealth Telecommunications.

Friday 16 — **"Minesweeping Favouritism"** East Coast holiday resorts are accusing the government of favouritism by clearing south coast beaches of mines first, saying no more than half their beaches will be open for Easter. The War Office say that they cannot spare any more trained mine detectors at present.

Saturday 17 — **"Back to Broadcasting"** The Director General of the BBC has claimed that regional broadcasting services across Europe will be back up and running within 90 days following the end of the war. Mr Haley stated that the work of the BBC has *'wiped Goebbels off the ether.'*

Sunday 18 — **"Stand down of NFS"** Over four thousand volunteer members of the National Fire Service were given their final inspection by the Home Secretary in Hyde Park before being permanently stood down. They marched past the Minister with military precision.

HERE IN BRITAIN

"The Most Hated Prison"

Dartmoor is to become a military 'glasshouse' and soldiers sentenced through court martial are to be sent there. Author Compton Mackenzie described the cells as *'Only 9ft by 5ft, the walls of undressed black granite down which the water trickles day and night.'* In such cells, it was said, *'the Dartmoor man spends seventeen hours out of twenty-four'*.

It is difficult to recruit warders to the gaol, situated, as an ex-convict wrote *'in a lonely part of the country, 1,100 feet above sea level, where it rains nine months in the year'*.

AROUND THE WORLD

"Blockbuster Crimean Conference"

A Moscow film showcasing the success of the Crimean Conference has been received well by the Russian public. Fans particularly enjoyed watching Churchill's thorough inspection of the Russian troops, looking each man in the eye, and seeing President Roosevelt tour the streets by US military Jeep.

Posters advertising the film show the flags of the three Allied powers, representing the unity forged at the Crimean and Yalta conferences. The film is intended to do more than just entertain, instead to educate the public, and strike fear into the retreating German forces.

ARMY OF VOLUNTEERS

Six representatives of the British Women's Voluntary Service have been invited by the French foreign office to visit the war-torn country, each staying with a family in a different area of France. The British women have expressed their horror at the lack of bare necessities available to villages and towns across the country, even in the most affluent of areas, and reported the situation back to the British government. The six will eventually join up in Paris to meet with similar French organisations.

The WVS, a separate organisation from that of the WAAF (Air Force) and the WRNS (Navy), was founded by the Marchioness of Reading, Stella Isaacs, who was originally asked to form a volunteer group of women to support the Air Raids Precaution Unit (ARP). Although this gave the WVS a reputation as an 'elitist' group, it nevertheless continued to grow between 1939 and 1941, when it was estimated to have over one million members. By this time, social class had no bearing on the group, with members of the aristocracy often working alongside cleaning ladies. The WVS outgrew its work as purely a support network to the ARP, and instead took instruction directly from the Government. By 1941, their government endorsed pamphlet, 'What Can You Do?' had encouraged the enlisting of many more women, previously constrained by societal expectations and the limiting factors of the patriarchy prevalent throughout Victorian Britain and the early 1900s.

Their work in coordinating evacuation from London, training civilians in air raid procedure and ensuring the maximum possible civil content proved to be invaluable, especially throughout the Blitz; they became familiar faces and authority figures within their respective communities. The WVS provided the country with a feeling of warmth and safety which even Churchill's great motivational war speeches could not.

MARCH 19TH - 25TH 1945

IN THE NEWS

Monday 19   **"Raising the School Age"** The Minister for Education has spoken of raising the required schooling age to 15, ahead of the original date of April 1947. However, this will be entirely dependent on the ability to recruit more teachers.

Tuesday 20   **"Neighbourly Lessons"** In an effort to 'break down the barriers' in new housing estates, social workers at Manchester University are training teachers to give lessons in friendliness. It is estimated that it will take at least five years to change the culture.

Wednesday 21   **"Western Front Hospital Visits"** For the first time since the beginning of the war, those who are seriously ill in hospitals on the Western Front, subject to conditions, are permitted to have two visitors each.

Thursday 22   **"A Return Home"** Areas in Sussex that have been off limits since 1940 are reopening. Permission has been granted to residents of the seaside towns of Winchelsea, Camber and Shoreham to return home.

Friday 23   **"Penny a Week Fund"** Mrs Churchill, speaking at the opening of the Red Cross 'Penny a Week' exhibition Railway Coach at King's Cross station, has said aid supplies sent to Russia have exceeded over 14,000 tons and £83,000.

Saturday 24   **"Hat Conscious"** Over 5 million cheap hats will be on sale for women in less than a year. Under a price restriction scheme, designed to make the public more 'hat conscious', the hats will be marked in shops with a star.

Sunday 25   **"Portraits Finished"** The full-length portraits of the King and Queen by Gerald Kelly, have at last been completed. Their majesties are shown wearing the jewels and gowns they wore at the coronation.

HERE IN BRITAIN

"Women At Work"

An investigation into the sickness records of over 20,000 women across munitions factories all over the country has yielded an interesting spread of results, that are being made a note of by the Medical Research Council. Interviews were conducted with several hundred women to discover that married women over the age of 35 are generally deemed to be more healthy, confident and 'less nervy' than single women around the same age. Not only this, but the older the married women, the better equipped they seemed to be able to 'stand up' to their bosses.

AROUND THE WORLD

"Dolls and 'Dolls'"

Goebbels' has issued a special order, to close Kruse's famous doll factory in Berlin on the grounds that since Frau Kruse's son was killed on the front line, 'she has produced all her dolls with very downcast and despairing facial expressions'. German officials are concerned about the effect on morale the dolls are having.

Because 'nobody looks at a woman's legs before lunch time,' Earl Constantine, the president of the American National Association of Hosiery Manufacturers, is asking women to go without stockings until noon, as rayon is in short supply.

Training in the highly dangerous coal industry was taken seriously. The Bevin's Boys had both theoretical and practical training in underground coal mining.

Twins were recently picked out in the same 'Bevin's Ballot'. *'Astronomical millions to one'* were the odds of both names to be drawn, and they didn't believe it. *'I think they've drawn one name and signed up both of us,'* and yet the Ministry of Labour insists that there has been no mistake. The ballot is done by randomly allocated numbers, not by name, and only then are the numbers traced to regional files.

The Bevin Ballot was introduced in 1944 when young men, aged 18 – 25, were first needed to be called up to work in the mines and they would be selected by ballot. Those whose National Service registration certificates end with the figure or figures, 0-9, drawn in the ballot by a Ministry of Labour clerk, are transferred to the coalmines. The 'victims' are Charlie and Herbert Chick, aged 18, of Lower Edmonton, Middlesex, *'Chicks out of the same hatch'*, says their mother, *'they didn't like it, they wanted to join the Army like their brothers'.*

The boys will be given at least four weeks training. 50% of their 44-hour week will be spent in physical training and classroom work, 30% on instruction below ground and the remaining 20% on surface work. An experienced miner will supervise their work during the first four weeks underground and (except in South Wales), they will not be sent to work at the coal face until they've have had at least four months underground experience. They will be billeted in a miner's home or in a specially built hostel and receive a minimum wage ranging from 39s 6d to 78s, with allowances for living away from home and when demobilisation comes, they will be dealt with exactly as though they were a soldier.

MARCH 26TH - APRIL 1ST 1945

IN THE NEWS

Monday 26   **"A Giant Amongst Giants"** Former Prime Minister, Earl Lloyd-George passed away peacefully at age 85 in Wales. Tributes have flooded in for the war time hero, who was *'in that war, what Winston Churchill is in this.'*

Tuesday 27   **"Scotland Yard or Hollywood?"** In a new venture by Scotland Yard, a short film entitled *'Man on the Beat'* has been making the rounds in partnership with the British Council. The film, depicting the daily life of being a 'bobby' has been a 'howling success' in 23 languages.

Wednesday 28   **"Toys for Britain Campaign"** The Lord Mayor of Melbourne has wasted no time in ensuring that the second 'Toys for Britain Campaign' is underway, following his disappointment that over 63,000 toys sent to Britain last year did not reach us in time for Christmas.

Thursday 29   **"No New Cars for Civilians"** The Ministry of War Transport has confirmed, no new cars will be on sale to civilians in the near future.

Friday 30   **"Lord Lloyd-George Funeral"** Lord Lloyd-George has been laid to rest next to the River Dwyfor, his favourite childhood playground. He will lie in a spinney which overlooks the river and the bridge on which he carved his initials 70 years ago.

Saturday 31   **"Rations Dependent on Harvest"** The Minister of Agriculture has made a strong appeal for volunteers for this years' harvest. Last year many potatoes and sugar beet were left to rot in the fields, leading to this year's shortage.

Sunday 1   **"Double Summertime Begins"** From tonight, Double Summertime will come into force, putting us two hours ahead of Greenwich Meantime. It will be in place until July 15th.

HERE IN BRITAIN

"Victory for The Motor Interests"

Following the war time record of 10,000 motoring deaths last year, the Pedestrian's Association is concerned that this figure will only continue to rise. With the publication of the report by the Ministry of War Transport proposing a 30-mph speed limit *'only to be applied with discretion'*, the Association is outraged and claims that the scheme is open to massive exploitation by drivers and traffic enforcers alike. In a statement, they commented that the report marks *'a victory for the motor interests in their campaign to weaken the enforcement of the law.'*

AROUND THE WORLD

"Mrs Churchill to Russia"

Mrs Churchill's Red Cross Aid to Russia Fund is to equip two hospitals, each of 500 beds, at Rostov-on-Don as a permanent memorial to the work of the fund.

The cost will be about £400,000, of which £200,000 - which will equip one of the hospitals - has been given by the Scottish branch of the British Red Cross Society.

At the invitation of the Soviet Government, Mrs Churchill is to visit Russia. She will go to Rostov to see the two hospitals, which are being rebuilt since they were devastated by the Germans.

MAUNDY MONEY

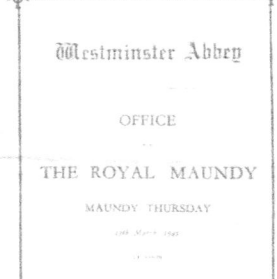

The distribution of Maundy Money, which takes place on the Thursday before Easter, is the modern development of an ancient ceremony said to be derived from when Christ washed his disciples' feet the evening before his crucifixion. In Britain the service goes back many centuries and Elizabeth I personally took part in 1572, in the hall at Greenwich. On that occasion a laundress, the sub-Almoner and the Lord High Almoner washed the feet of the poor people, and the feet then being, apparently, thoroughly clean, were again washed and kissed by the Queen herself. She then distributed broadcloth for the making of clothes and fish, bread and wine. Royalty continued to take part but the last time the foot-washing ritual took place was in 1685. Several changes have taken place since then. Clothing was substituted for broadcloth for the women but that was stopped in 1724 and money was given in lieu. In 1837 William IV agreed to give the pensioners thirty shillings in lieu of all provisions.

For many years the ceremony took place in Whitehall Chapel moving later to Westminster Abbey. This year the King distributed the Maundy money and the Queen was present, seated in the sacrarium of the Abbey. In addition to banknotes and cash (including a crown piece) which have now taken the place of all other forms of gift, the pensioners receive some of the world's most interesting coins presented in a small leather purse, with as many pence as the monarch has years of age. The recipients themselves number as many men and as many women as the monarch has years. In the days before base metal money, the amount was made up from silver pennies, twopences, threepences and fourpences and are still, today, struck in silver and polished like proof coins.

APRIL 2ND – 8TH 1945

IN THE NEWS

Monday 2

thieves

"**Black Market Bloom**" Nurserymen across Norfolk are protecting their bulb growing fields against an ever-increasing onslaught of black-market thieves. Farmers report stealing up to 500 daffodils.

Tuesday 3

"**Woman Police Magistrate**" The King has approved a recommendation by the Home Secretary for a female Metropolitan Police Magistrate, for the first time ever.

Wednesday 4

"**Patience is a Virtue**" Evacuees who left areas of Greater London at the beginning of the war have been told to '*stay patient*' until formal notice is given to return. The Government has promised that as soon as the time is right, the go ahead will be given.

Thursday 5

"**5,000 Packs of Smokes**" As onlookers watched on desperately, the equivalent of 5,000 years' worth of one man's cigarettes were reduced to ashes at a NAAFI store in Skelmorlie, Scotland. Valued at over £150,000, the cigarettes were destroyed when a fire caused the explosion of matches within the shop.

Friday 6

"**International Airbase Competition**" First place and a prize of £500 has been awarded to a team of designers for their combined land-plane and flying-boat airport that would take up around 243 square miles. The airport will have an expected life of 15-20 years.

Saturday 7

"**Royal Football Fans**" The King, Queen and Princess Elizabeth were all present to witness Chelsea win the Football League War Cup South when they beat Millwall in the final 2–0.

Sunday 8

"**Free News**" The BBC yearbook, the sixth of the war, is being transmitted in German from liberated Luxembourg as a means of propaganda against the Nazis. Amongst the stories being told are the real causes of the war.

HERE IN BRITAIN

"Boys Behaving Badly"

The rise of cases being seen by the Juvenile Courts has been attributed to a lack of positive male role models for boys. Whilst it would be assumed that, with fathers of early adolescent teens being away on the continent, the schoolmaster would assume the role of positive influence, this has not been the case.

Over 20,000 teachers are serving in the armed forces, leaving the majority of teaching roles to be fulfilled by women. Whilst no less competent in ability, the positive effect of male authority on young men has been made apparent.

AROUND THE WORLD

"Hidden Treasure"

Bullion valued at £15,000, which was buried by Colonel Charles Smith in April 1942 as the Japanese advanced on the island of Panay in the Philippines, has been recovered. It took two days to uncover the gold from the basement of a warehouse where the Japanese had stored molasses.

That had melted when the city was set on fire during the later American occupation, forming a six-inch layer above the floor. The Filipinos who did the digging did not know what they were digging for, '*and their eyes opened wide when they saw the gold.*'

BIDDENDEN MAIDS

On Easter Monday morning, the village of Biddenden in Kent is the scene of a curious old custom called the Biddenden Maids' Charity. In normal times, tea, cheese and loaves of bread are given to the local widows and pensioners from the window of the Old Workhouse. Large amounts of Biddenden Cakes, baked of flour and water, so hard as to be inedible to allow better preservation as souvenirs, are distributed among the crowd of tourists and spectators, each cake bearing the effigy of the Biddenden Maids, two women whose bodies appear to be joined together.

According to tradition, Mary and Eliza Chulkhurst, were born to fairly wealthy parents in 1100 and their bodies were joined at the hips and shoulders. Although, by necessity, close friends, one source states that they sometimes disagreed in minor matters, and had 'frequent quarrels, which sometimes terminated in blows.' In 1134, after 34 years, Mary was suddenly taken ill and died and it was suggested that Eliza should be separated from her sister's corpse by a surgical operation, but she refused with the words, *"As we came together, we will also go together"*, and herself died six hours later. It is from this point that Biddenden's charitable tradition supposedly started - with the sisters pledging the profits from the 20 acres of land they owned be used to provide a dole of bread, cheese and beer to the poor each Easter.

Doubts have been cast on the truth of the old legend, but there is still a demand for the cakes and the bread — made to the archaic quartern loaf size - although in this wartime year of rationing, the cheese has been substituted with cocoa. True or not, the wrought iron village sign shows the Biddenden Maids.

IN THE NEWS

Monday 9   **"The Princess Put to Work"** The King and Queen, accompanied by Princess Margaret, visited the ATS Mechanical Transport training centre, where they watched as Princess Elizabeth, dressed in blue overalls, was hard at work mending an army lorry.

Tuesday 10   **"Rest in Peace"** A memorial service honouring the late David Lloyd George, former wartime Prime Minister, took place in Westminster Abbey. The Service was even better attended, as many international and Commonwealth statesmen were already in London for a conference.

Wednesday 11   **"The Commonwealth Conference"** Commonwealth leaders were amongst many other state officials who gathered in Westminster today to discuss the formation of a World Security Council. The event was organised by the Empire Parliamentary Association.

Thursday 12   **"Death of a President"** In unexpected and sudden circumstances, President Roosevelt has died at age 63. The four-time elected President has been statistically voted the most popular ever, and his death will leave a hole in the heart of Americans across the country.

Friday 13   **"Victory for the Scots"** For the first time ever, a representative from the Scottish National Party will sit in the House of Commons; Robert McIntyre secured victory in the Motherwell By-Election.

Saturday 14   **"Tock Tick"** With the village church clock continually puzzling the inhabitants of Swaffham in Norfolk, a nest of jackdaws was discovered in its inner workings. A work order has been approved for their removal.

Sunday 15   **"Australian Immigration"** Many of the 3,000 dock workers who have been shipped to Australia to help maintain the British fleet stationed out there, have commented that they would like to stay in the country after the war.

HERE IN BRITAIN
"'Rubbishy' War-Time Toys"

The British Toy Manufacturers Association has finally shed light on the long unanswered question of the conspicuous reduction in quality of toys being produced and sold over the last few years.

Somewhat predictably,the war effort even targets Britain's most passive industries as most of the toy manufacturing companies switched to war production very soon after 1939 and have been on war 'duty' since. They hope a return to normal is imminent, and British toys can return to the quality and appeal of their pre-war status.

AROUND THE WORLD
"Anxious Wives v Coastguard"

The US Coastguard have reported that the primary hindrance to their surveillance for German U-Boats has been the large number of *'anxious housewives'* who ring to report their husbands missing, after not returning at their expected time. Rather than fighting with enemy vessels, the men more often than not, get carried away with beer and poker aboard pleasure ships, and are merely returning later than originally stated. The Coastguard has warned wives not to contact them unless their husbands are missing for a very long time.

UNLUCKY FOR SOME!

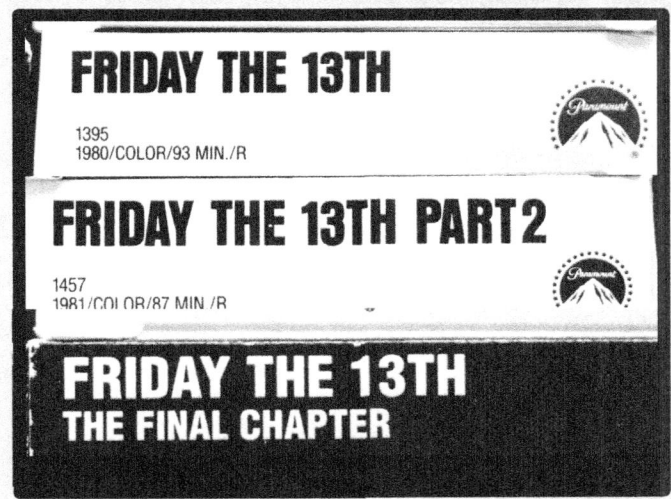

This ship has no deck 13.

Hot Glass Show	15
Oceanview Café	14
Staterooms	12
Staterooms	11

The ominous Friday 13th has struck again, in its usual unlucky fashion, as seventeen greyhounds, meant to be racing the following day, fell unanimously ill before their big race. The event, meant to be held at the White City Stadium, with over 5,000 spectators, had to be cancelled. It is safe to assume that the organisers were not best pleased and will be wary of the date before holding another event.

The number 13 and Friday both have an individual long history of bringing bad luck. In the Bible, Judas, who betrayed Jesus, was the 13th guest to sit down to the Last Supper. In Norse mythology, a dinner party of the gods was ruined by the 13th guest called Loki, 'god of deceit and evil', who caused the world to be plunged into darkness. Peoples of the Mediterranean, regarded 13 with suspicion, not being as perfect as 12, which is divisible in many ways.

As for 'Friday', according to tradition, Adam and Eve were expelled from Eden; Cain murdered Abel; St John the Baptist was beheaded the enactment of the order of Herod for the massacre of the innocents, all took place on a Friday. In Chaucer's Canterbury Tales, written in the 14th Century, he says 'and on a Friday fell all this mischance'. Here in Britain, Friday was once known as 'Hangman's Day' because it was usually when people who had been condemned to death would be hanged and the great crash of 1869, when the price of gold plummeted, was on Friday too.

Whilst some would call it irrational, it is common for people to have *'Paraskavidekatriaphobia,'* which is the name for a fear of Friday 13th. This condition may have arisen in the White City Stadium event organisers after the events of the weekend.

APRIL 16TH - 22ND 1945

IN THE NEWS

Monday 16   **"Turn the Heat Off"** Summer is here, or so the Government is trying the persuade the British people, as the recent warm weather led Parliament to ban central heating in shops, factories, offices, and theatres.

Tuesday 17   **"V-Day Drive"** Confidence in the war effort has reached an all-time high, as the King and Queen practiced the procession that will be made on V-Day, from Buckingham Palace to St Paul's Cathedral by horse drawn coach.

Wednesday 18   **"The Wimpey"** The last air raid of the Wellington Bomber, affectionately nicknamed '*The Wimpey*' by RAF crews, has been made against railway yards in Northern Italy. The aircraft has been active since the beginning of the war.

Thursday 19   **"97th Archbishop of Canterbury"** The former Archbishop of London, Dr Geoffrey Fisher, has today been inaugurated as the 97th Archbishop of Canterbury in a special ceremony at Canterbury Cathedral.

Friday 20   **"Expensive Crashes"** Road accidents cost the country over £50 million per year, reported Lord Brabazon at the Roadfarers' Club lunch. The Parliamentary Secretary to the Minister of War Transport has said that he will not dispute this number, but appealed for acceptance of the proposed post war restrictions.

Saturday 21   **"Eggstra-ordinary Record"** The Ministry of Food's Director of Egg Supplies has reported that he hopes to make 39 to 40 allocations of eggs this year compared to the 30 last year. This follows a record delivery of over 22 million eggs from Canada.

Sunday 22   **"Forces Only"** A factory is to be set up in North Wales that will employ, exclusively, ex-servicemen after the end of the war, as an offer of thanks.

HERE IN BRITAIN

"Penicillin in the Air"

Penicillin via inhalation is the new idea emerging from medical professionals. In a report, this alternative method was stated as a possible means for more effective and efficient administration of the drug, which currently is via injection.

It was even proposed that a small ward would possibly be able to be kept under a constant state of sedation with the air being filled with penicillin for sustained periods of time. The technique would not only be more effective in pain relief, but also use less of the drug than injection.

AROUND THE WORLD

"Not V-Day for All"

In a speech this week, the Australian Deputy Prime Minister said, '*V-Day is not the end*', reminding the British Government of the persisting threat of Japan.

Although the people of Australia will be as happy as those in Europe about the end of the war against the Nazis, it is important not to underestimate the strength of the Japanese, against whom British forces are currently engaged in Burma and across the Pacific Ocean. On V-Day there will be thousands of British men and women thinking of their loved ones still fighting in Asia.

THE WINDMILL THEATRE

REMEMBERING
Revudeville

1932 - 1964

A SOUVENIR OF THE
WINDMILL THEATRE

Compiled by Jill Millard Shapiro

First opened in 1931, and becoming the centre of non-stop revue in 1932, London's Windmill Theatre is to be closed. The theatre's well-known slogan throughout the Blitz was *'We will never close'* but now, 33 years after its inaugural show, the curtains will close for the last time and whilst the traditional theatre, most recently owned by Sheila Van Damm, daughter of the founder, will go, the premises will reopen next week as a cinema.

Based in Piccadilly, The Windmill was founded by socialite Laura Henderson, a widow who inherited a fortune after the death of her wealthy husband, and her business partner and producer theatre impresario Vivian Van Damm and she managed to negotiate with the Lord Chamberlain to amend centuries-old laws to allow women to perform nude on the stage. With his permission, Windmill Theatre manager, Van Damm, began immediately to introduce by 1932 his *tableaux vivants*. Inspired by the Folies Bergère, nude or scantily draped women with the instruction *'if you move, it's rude'* were surrounded by elaborate moving sets while dancers whirled and wafted large feather fans. The feather fans used to conceal - or reveal - their nudity. The famous troupe of Bluebell Girls were favourite dancers at the Windmill. The troupe of precision dancers, all more than 5' 9" tall, were founded by Margaret Kelly, who was professionally called Miss 'Bluebell' to reflect her piercing blue eyes. From these motionless tableaux, the famous 'fan dance' was created.

The venue eventually evolved into the home of the variety show, where stars like Bruce Forsyth, Peter Sellers and Tony Hancock honed their acts, and although the girls remained the biggest draw, Spike Milligan, Peter Sellers, Bruce Forsyth and Barry Cryer were among those that had their first success at the Windmill.

APRIL 23RD - 29TH 1945

IN THE NEWS

Monday 23   **"Shrewsbury Limes Felled"** The famous lime trees in Shrewsbury Quarry have been condemned as dangerous and permission has been given for them to be felled. Originally planted in 1719, some of the trees now reach over 100ft tall.

Tuesday 24   **"Big Ben to Shine Again"** To the cheering of a small crowd of onlookers, and those inside the Houses of Parliament, Big Ben's lantern has been reignited for the first time since the beginning of the war.

Wednesday 25   **"Anzac Day"** The King delivered his annual address to the people of Australia on Anzac Day. The celebrations commemorate the efforts of Australian servicemen and their help to the British over centuries of warfare.

Thursday 26   **"Still More Light"** Pre-war lighting is now being allowed in trains, trams, and buses in the greater part of the country, but restrictions are still necessary in the coastal areas to avoid helping enemy submarines.

Friday 27   **"Houses in Crates"** The first of the 30,000 temporary houses being delivered to Britain under the lend lease arrangements with America have been delivered.

Saturday 28   **"Mussolini Dead"** Former Italian dictator, Mussolini, has been executed by Italian Partisans, along with twelve other members of his former cabinet, after being caught attempting to flee across the Swiss border. Their bodies were carried through Milan on public display.

Sunday 29   **"Petrol Rations"** Basic petrol ration coupons have been printed and are ready for any decision about the restoration of the basic ration or other relaxations of the petrol rationing, that the Government might make after the end of the European war.

HERE IN BRITAIN

"Shakespeare's Birthday"

As annual celebrations in Stratford Upon Avon commenced to celebrate the birthday of Britain's most famous playwright, an influx of American's flocked to the town to join in the festivities. Americans, even more so than in peace time, were incredibly enthusiastic about the event, with a US military band playing in the high street before the mayor's speech and the formal procession from Shakespeare's house to the town square. It was also announced that 1944 saw record admissions to the Shakespeare Memorial Theatre, almost exceeding 200,000.

AROUND THE WORLD

"GB to AUS In 24 Hours"

'The invention of jet-propelled aircraft should facilitate the journey between England and Australia in under 24 hours by 1960'. These were the words of Qantas Empire Airways' Managing Director, Mr Fysh, who is confident that jet and gas propulsion will revolutionise air travel.

He said that Great Britain leads the United Nations in the development of this new flight. The first of five Lancastrian air liners for the Sydney-London service arrived at Sydney completing the trip in 58 flying hours.

FOOD FOR OUR TROOPS

Army rations are sufficient, if there is no waste, to supply troops with four good meals a day -breakfast, mid-day, tea and supper - but meals are not good unless they are well cooked and served hot. Army chefs and instructors all attend the Army Catering Corps Training Centre at Aldershot where the equipment is equal to that of the best hotels. Before the outbreak of war, expert caterers were placed in key positions as advisers to the Army, and when war began, their number was increased by the granting of emergency reserve commissions to caterers with the requisite qualifications. About 40,000 men have already taken the Aldershot courses and by the end of the war, the three services together will probably have trained as many as 100,000 cooks.

However, field service conditions bear no resemblance to those of an ideal training centre. Army cooks must know a good deal besides cooking with the latest appliances, and Aldershot is not training cooks for the catering industry - although many thousands will be competent to take good places in the industry after the war - but for the army in barracks, in camps and on the field of war where the cook will often have to improvise. Training is done in the open-air as well as in the kitchen and here the students learn to use portable camp equipment such as Bluff and Triplex ranges and Soyer stoves, improvised oil-drum ovens and the primitive kettle trench. The Army also uses hay and insulator boxes in which food brought to cooking heat over a fire will finish cooking in a moving lorry while the unit is on the march. The Army Catering Corps is a combatant corps and in appreciation of the services of its cooks, the Army awards them extra pay.

IN THE NEWS

Monday 30   **"Out Like a Lion"** Severe snowstorms saw off April 1945, as the worst storm for 50 years swept across Dover. Within an hour, over three inches of snow covered the ground and by midday this figure had doubled.

Tuesday 1   **"Hitler is Dead"** Grand Admiral Donitz, the self-appointed successor to Adolf Hitler, announced the death of the Fuhrer on German national radio in the early hours of the morning. The German dictator shot himself whilst hiding in his bunker as news of allied forces advancing on Berlin reached High Command.

Wednesday 2   **"Surprise Strike"** Without any warning, over 4,300 tram, trolly and bus men refused to go on duty this morning, in a surprise strike that crippled public transport across the Capital. On some other routes the crews of the vehicles were 'working to rule', so that those services were delayed too.

Thursday 3   **"The Final Bell"** The very last 'all clear' siren has been sounded, and with it ends 5 years of siren and noise regulation with no prohibition on hooters, sirens and rattles.

Friday 4   **"Coventry Cathedral"** Two drawings have been exhibited showcasing the design of the new Coventry Cathedral. They incorporate the remains of the pre-war building, which sustained irreparable damage during German air raids.

Saturday 5   **"Portrait Paradise"** This summer's Royal Academy public exhibition will contain many portraits, including two official pieces of the King and Queen.

Sunday 6   **"Anonymous BBC"** The announcer's name on BBC news broadcasts, introduced in 1940 as a war time security measure, will no longer be necessary for future programmes.

HERE IN BRITAIN

"Saving Telephones"

The steps taken by the Post Office to minimise the damage to telephone services at the beginning of the war can now be revealed by the Ministry of Defence. Many vital defence lines were run underneath street level, in tube lines and other fabricated deep tunnels created by Post Office engineers.

Over 1,200 trunk circuits were connected to a centralised exchange and covered with concrete so thick that it was considered bomb proof. Six other centres on the outskirts of London, were constructed as a fail safe in the event of a central failure.

AROUND THE WORLD

"End of The Dictator"

Few men in history can be attributed to more destruction than the exploits of Adolf Hitler, who committed suicide earlier this week. The *'house painter turned master of Europe'* will go down infamously in the history books for plunging Europe, and subsequently the world, into a never-before-seen period of destruction.

From the time he became master of Germany he made lies, cruelty, and terror his principal means to achieve his ideal of the Third Reich, and he has become in the eyes of virtually the whole world an incarnation of absolute evil.

MAY DAY TRADITIONS

A wheel of cheese in the Randwick Wap ceremony (inset) and Maypole dancing (main).

May Day is a celebration of spring and many of the associated festivities date back to early Medieval times. The 1st of May was traditionally the start of 'Mary's Month' or a month of Christian devotions to the Virgin Mary and was usually declared a holiday allowing everyone to enjoy their inevitable local fair and festivities.

At Oxford's Magdalen Bridge, crowds still gather at first light to hear the May Singing of a hymn, and a madrigal by the choristers of Magdalen College. Later in the day, local Morris dancers entertain those out and about in the city's main streets. In the Gloucestershire village of Randwick, an ancient ceremony known as the Randwick Wap dates back to the 14th century. The Wap is a fair, with a rowdy procession in costume. Three wheels of cheese are elaborately decorated and carried in the procession before being rolled three times round the churchyard. It is an occasion for much quaffing of ale and wine, and although banned in the Victorian period as 'too rowdy and boozy' it was enthusiastically revived two years ago.

Central to most May Day celebrations is the Maypole, which at one time was a large tree in the forest that was decorated in situ, but later was cut down and brought into the village to be decorated with flowers, wreaths, handkerchiefs and ribbons. Complicated dances are performed around it while holding the ribbons attached to the top, which then weave a colourful braid pattern down the length of the pole. During the 16th and 17th centuries, many of the famous village maypoles were destroyed and the celebrations banned as being 'occasions of sin'. However, the late 19th century saw a renewed interest in English customs and May Day became a fixture in the calendar once more.

MAY 7TH - 13TH 1945

IN THE NEWS

Monday 7   **"Unconditional Surrender"** The German Foreign Minister broadcast the following announcement: *'German men and women, the high command of the armed forces has to-day, at the order of Grand Admiral Donitz, declared the unconditional surrender of all fighting German troops.'*

Tuesday 8   **"Biggest Crowd"** The largest ever crowd, eclipsing even the Coronation and the Silver Jubilee, gathered outside Buckingham Palace following the news of the German surrender. Chants of *'we want the King'* were heard outside the gates.

Wednesday 9   **"Coastal Black-Out"** The coastal black-out must remain active reported the Admiralty *'with regret'* until it can be confirmed that all U-Boats have been given, and received, the order to surrender; the restrictions will be removed as soon as possible.

Thursday 10   **"The Last Act of Surrender"** The final act of ratification certifying the German surrender was signed in Berlin at a ceremonial midnight meeting between the Allied Expeditionary force, the Russian High Command and the German High Command.

Friday 11   **"Diamonds for Mrs Churchill"** The Soviet Foreign Minister's wife gave Mrs Churchill a diamond ring adorned with a gold pectoral cross and encrusted with jewels. She said, *'I hope this ring will continue to gleam as a bright symbol of Anglo-Soviet friendship.'*

Saturday 12   **"Bevin's Ballot"** 'Bevin's boys,' as those selected from the young mine workers ballot have been affectionately nicknamed, will cease following the suspension of the programme which has run for 16 months.

Sunday 13   **"The Nation Gives Thanks"** An emotional thanksgiving service was held at St Paul's Cathedral and attended by the King and Queen; the Archbishop of Canterbury, who led the service, called for this *'national thanksgiving'.*

HERE IN BRITAIN

"Delay Means Holiday"

After five years, eight months and four days of the bloodiest war in history, Britain and her allies have gained victory in Europe. Capitulation of Germany to the Allies was announced by Donitz on 7th May, but a technicality in the arrangements made with Russia and America as to when the victory was to be announced, delayed the British people's celebration. One happy result is that Britain's workers had two clear days' holiday—the 8th and 9th of May. The announcement made late at night stated that *the 8th of May* was VE-Day.

AROUND THE WORLD

"How They Celebrated in NY"

The news of the German unconditional surrender earlier this week brought large crowds onto the streets of New York, rejoicing at the end of the war in Europe. Whilst large numbers of American troops are still deployed across Asia and the Pacific in the ongoing conflict against the Japanese, Times Square was nevertheless filled to such an extent that police were forced to shut down traffic and tramlines through the district. Even after police shut down the crowds, people could be seen praying in doorways and at their windows.

VE DAY CELEBRATIONS

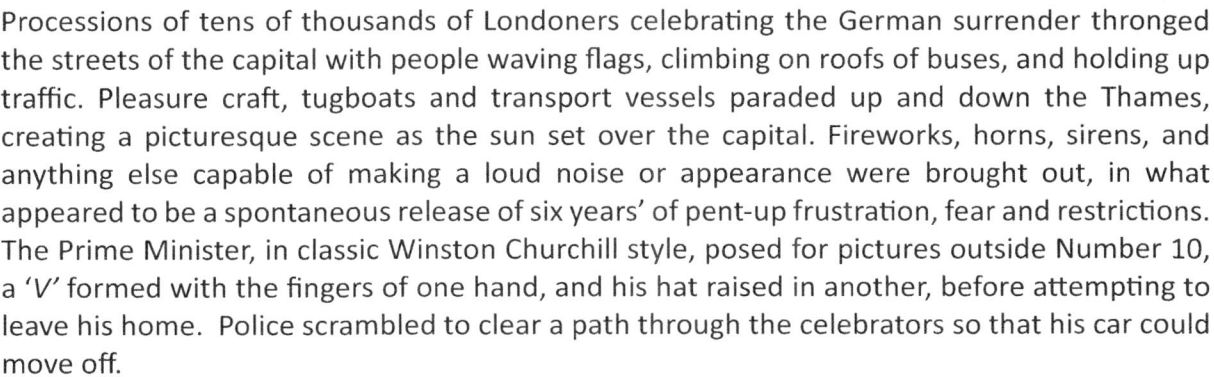

Processions of tens of thousands of Londoners celebrating the German surrender thronged the streets of the capital with people waving flags, climbing on roofs of buses, and holding up traffic. Pleasure craft, tugboats and transport vessels paraded up and down the Thames, creating a picturesque scene as the sun set over the capital. Fireworks, horns, sirens, and anything else capable of making a loud noise or appearance were brought out, in what appeared to be a spontaneous release of six years' of pent-up frustration, fear and restrictions. The Prime Minister, in classic Winston Churchill style, posed for pictures outside Number 10, a 'V' formed with the fingers of one hand, and his hat raised in another, before attempting to leave his home. Police scrambled to clear a path through the celebrators so that his car could move off.

One of each flag from every Allied Nation could be seen in all London districts, and celebrations were especially joyous in areas most severely affected by the war. Damage sustained during bombing raids to so many London suburbs served to only fuel the jubilation of their people, as queues for the bakers, butchers and confectionery stores stretched 'round the block'. As a national holiday was declared for both the 8th and 9th, Sunday transport services were instigated, with extra trains put on to carry the inevitable huge influx of people to the capital, where the 'half-hearted efforts' of police to control the crowds meant that, for the first time in six years, people were able to fully enjoy themselves.

IN THE NEWS

Monday 14   "Demob the Mothers" Amid claims that only a mother can *'make a house a home,'* the Minister of Labour has been advised to *'demob the mothers'* from industry so that they might return home to be with their children.

Tuesday 15   "Swamped by Fish and Chips" Grimsby has received so much fish that more workers have been recruited to process and handle it all. Danish and Swedish fishing boats have landed over 14 thousand boxes already and a further 70 vessels are waiting.

Wednesday 16   "Eisenhower 'On Leave'" General Eisenhower enjoyed the *'nicest night [he's] had since the war started'* when he watched a performance of 'Strike it Again' in a London theatre. He was surrounded by a happy 'scrimmage' at his car when he left.

Thursday 17th   "Royal Family in Edinburgh" Scottish celebrations for the Allied victory reached their climax in Edinburgh when the city was visited by the Royal Family. In their honour, the principal buildings in Edinburgh were floodlit for the first time since 1939.

Friday 18th   "Teacher Training College" Following the war time shortage of teachers from pre-school to secondary level, over 8,000 candidates have already been shortlisted for teacher training colleges across the country,

Saturday 19   "Shakespeare Festival" A pageant performed by local school children and civil defence members, followed by a service in Southwark Cathedral, had a surprise visit from the Queen and Princess Elizabeth.

Sunday 20   "Royal Salute" More than 6,000 members of the British Legion, primarily bemedaled veterans of the First World War, spearheaded a two-mile-long procession through London from the Cenotaph to Buckingham Palace where the King took the salute.

HERE IN BRITAIN

"Dresses From Curtains"

'Make do and mend' is having its 'last hurrah' as women across the country are scrambling to put together outfits suitable for victory celebrations. Curtains have been transformed into light summer dresses, and black out blinds, following the end of 'dim out', have been dealt 'good riddance' and made into Hungarian style skirts embroidered round the hems with gaily coloured wool. Laundered 'flower bags' (2s 6d and 3s) are in demand for another fashion. Women are making them into summer pants for their husbands. One bag makes one pair and saves three coupons.

AROUND THE WORLD

"Boston's Fourth Centenary"

The town of Boston celebrated its fourth centenary since being granted its charter of incorporation by Henry VIII, with a special meeting of the Town Council.

In attendance was Lord Huntingfield who, on behalf of his cousin, Mr Allan Forbes of Boston, Massachusetts accepted an honorary *'freedom of the borough scroll'* as a gesture of friendship between the two areas and in appreciation of his efforts to foster friendship between the two Bostons. The scroll of freedom, engrossed on vellum was placed in a casket made from 15th century oak from Boston Stump.

PRINCESS 'MAY' OF TECK

The Coronation of King George V

There was a particularly affectionate welcome for Queen Mary, 78 this month, at the thanksgiving service in St Paul's, where she was seen on her first ceremonial occasion in London since before the war. The King had been worried about his mother's safety during the conflict and suggested that she move to the country where it would be safer. She did what he asked and went to live with her niece, the Duchess of Beaufort at Badminton Park, from where she offered lifts to soldiers, visited hospitals and took part in the war effort.

Queen Mary was born Victoria Mary Augusta Louise Olga Pauline Claudine Agnes Mary in Kensington Palace in 1867 to Duke Francis and Duchess Mary of Teck. Young Mary, known as May, is the great-granddaughter of George III and a second cousin to Queen Victoria. At the behest of Queen Victoria, Mary was engaged to Queen Victoria's grandson Prince Albert Victor but he died shortly afterwards. Queen Victoria suggested that Mary marry Albert's brother George and although it was an arranged marriage, George and Mary fell deeply in love. When Queen Victoria died, Mary's father-in-law became King Edward VII and when he died, George became King George V and Mary was his Queen for 25 years. Her eldest son Edward became Edward VIII after the death of his father and on Edward's shocking abdication to marry Wallis Simpson, her second son, Albert, became our present King George VI.

The Dowager Queen Mary devotes herself to many charities but is also known for wearing several dazzling pieces of jewellery all at one time. She might wear several necklaces, brooches, stomachers, bracelets, rings and of course a crown, often mixing diamonds, pearls, emeralds, sapphires and rubies. She is sometimes criticised for her keen acquisition of 'objets d'art' for the Royal Collection – she has been known to express to hosts that she admires something in their possession, in the expectation that they would be willing to donate it!

MAY 21ST - 27TH 1945

IN THE NEWS

Monday 21   **"Carefree Bank Holiday"** For the first time for many since 1939, today marked the first carefree bank holiday since the end of the war. Reports came in showing there was enjoyment almost on pre-war levels.

Tuesday 22   **"Empire Air Navigation School"** RAF Flying Command's Empire Air Navigation School has successfully flown the British built Lancaster aircraft 'Aries' over the North Magnetic Pole, from an airbase in northern Canada.

Wednesday 23   **"Caretaker Government"** Prime Minister Winston Churchill officially ended the wartime coalition government and announced a 'caretaker' Conservative government pending a general election.

Thursday 24   **"Empire Day"** Empire Day was celebrated across the country with principal events in all major cities. A tea party organised by the King and Queen at Buckingham Palace for repatriated prisoners of war was a highlight.

Friday 25   **"French Honours for Monty"** Field Marshall Montgomery has become one of the few foreigners to be honoured with the title *'Grand Cross of the Legion of Honour.'* The ceremony was held in the courtyard of the 'Invalides', in Paris.

Saturday 26   **"Navy Lags Behind"** The ongoing demands of the war in the Pacific against the Japanese means that discharges from the Royal Navy will be far fewer, and far later, than those from the other armed services, especially those in 'Group One,' the men over 50.

Sunday 27   **"More Lifeboats"** During the war, production of lifeboats practically ceased as resources were redirected to the war effort, which left Britain's RNLI severely lacking. Over £800,000 has now been allocated for the construction of new vessels and equipment.

HERE IN BRITAIN

"Battle of the Magnetic Mine"

Hitler's first *'secret weapon'* of the war, the *'magnetic mine,'* and how the Allies managed to neutralise its threat has at last been released in a story by the Ministry of Defence. Throughout the early period of the war, several techniques were tested including flat fish fitted with magnets and giant coils attached to aircraft, all yielding no success; it was eventually the *'Double L'* method, involving two minesweeper ships each towing a long line of live electrical cables, that could successfully create enough current to de-activate the bombs within a 10-acre radius.

AROUND THE WORLD

"Shakespeare Returns to the Rock"

With a *'terrifically vital'* performance of Twelfth Night, Shakespeare returned to Gibraltar for the first time in over a century. It was March 28th, 1842 that *'the celebrated juvenile actress Miss Davenport, who was presented with the last hat worn by the late Kean after her performance in London'* appeared in Richard the Third on the island, after *'having reposed in Italy from her extraordinary efforts as dramatic star in America.'* The present production by all ranks of all services, has been produced by a *'debating society founded by the more serious-minded troops in 1941'.*

WHITSUNTIDE

This month, Whit Sunday was celebrated around the world by Catholics, Anglicans and Methodists. This special day is celebrated to commemorate the descent of the Holy Spirit upon Christ's disciples and is the seventh day after Easter or Pentecost, its name deriving from the Anglo-Saxon word 'wit' meaning 'understanding' to celebrate the disciples being filled with the wisdom of the Holy Spirit.

Whit Monday was officially recognised as a bank holiday in 1871 and the day has a special cultural significance in the north-west of England. Many workplaces including factories and cotton mills closed for the whole Whitsuntide week giving workers a holiday and towns held fairs, markets, and parades. Still a major tradition is the 'Whit Walk', when local churches or chapels employ bands to lead traditional processions through the streets. Often the Catholic Sunday schools walk on Whit Friday and the Anglican Sunday schools on Whit Monday bringing in an element of competition in display, dresses and banners! The origin of these processions date back to July 1821 when the children of Manchester commemorated the coronation of George IV and children of all denominations walked in procession from their schools and assembled at Ardwick Green to sing 'God Save the King'.

The Bradford Whit Walk has been held continuously since 1903 and is one of the most popular events on the race-walking calendar, attracting hundreds of entries. At the height of its popularity, it attracted top British race walkers and in the 20s and 30s was recognised as the breeding ground for British Olympians, with winners Tommy Green and Harold Whitlock going on to win Olympic gold medals in 1932 and 1936 respectively. This is also the week for many local brass band contests and workers to take the opportunity to enjoy canal boat rides, go to the races and of course, go to the seaside.

MAY 28TH - JUNE 3RD 1945

IN THE NEWS

Monday 28   **"North Pole"** Over 17,000 miles of flights have been devoted to finding the true position of the magnetic North Pole. This has now been achieved, it is believed, from recordings taken by Britain's Lancaster Aries on a 4,000 mile, non-stop, flight over the area.

Tuesday 29   **"Kipper Day"** Kippers for tea may well be the rule again as people queued and waited to to buy them from shops across the country for the first time in many months.

Wednesday 30   **"US Memorial Day"** American soldiers, both in Europe and at home, paid homage to fallen soldiers from both the First and Second World Wars on their official Memorial Day. The American Ambassador placed a wreath on the tomb of the unknown soldier at Westminster Abbey.

Thursday 31   **"Wakes Weeks"** Special arrangements have been proposed for those in Lancashire towns who may be on holiday on election day. The famous *'wakes weeks'* are familiar to the Prime Minister, who was once MP for Oldham.

Friday 1   **"Lawton Coming South"** Football star Tommy Lawton, with over 30 caps for England, is set to make a shock move from Everton to a London Soccer Club. Everton paid £7,000 for the then 17-year-old in 1936.

Saturday 2   **"Colonial Service Vacancies"** Large scale recruitment schemes for the Colonial Office have resumed now that the war is over; more than 4,000 vacancies exist for technical appointments for reconstruction in the Colonies.

Sunday 3   **"Return of Queen Mary"** Crowds lined the streets of Bristol to see Queen Mary make her last journey from her war time residence in Badminton back to her home at Marlborough House in London.

HERE IN BRITAIN

"Like Turkey Cocks"

Housewives in Cambridge prepared and packed the rations which would have kept the British North Pole flyers alive if they had been forced down in the Arctic.

Breakfast would have been porridge with eggs or fish; lunch, stewed meat, fish, pie or curry, with fruit or semolina pudding; and supper, meat and vegetables, with soup or pudding, plus, tea, cocoa, sweets or chocolate. Most of the food was dehydrated, and the flyers would need petrol for cooking it and snow or ice to provide water for mixing. They could *'feast like Turkey Cocks.'*

AROUND THE WORLD

"A Hair in My Food"

Human hair is an unlikely waste product to be recycled and re-purposed, but, scarcely imaginable, hair, especially cleaner, ladies' hair, from barbers and hairdressers has the potential to be turned into food high in nutrients to give strength to premature babies and malnourished people. The technique, involving the extraction of 'cystine' from the roots, which is a kind of pre-digested food, is already used for those starving in Europe, and for liberated French prisoners of war, to help regain their strength. Cystine's future potential is to be processed as a medicine.

LOOTED VALUABLES FOUND

*German troops loot a painting from a church.
Eisenhower inspects a hoard of art discovered
hidden in a salt mine after the war.*

The American 88th Division has the unusual task of not only dismantling some 600,000 German troops, but also guarding one of the largest collections of miscellaneous valuables that has ever existed. The Americans' job is to aid in the demobilisation of the Fourteenth German army, along with liberating and re-homing thousands of refugees from concentration camps in the province of Alto Adige. Being nearer the back of the German lines, the area received a large amount of the loot recovered from occupied cities, where it has stayed and built up into quite the collection. Amongst the *'left luggage'* there are some 8 railway trucks filled to the brim with gold bars, the Italian Crown Jewels, over one million Italian paper lira and King Victor Emmanuel's prized collection of coins. Just one of these inventories is estimated to be worth at least £750 million, and there are more than a dozen dotted across the country.

Safe deposit rooms have been hinted at by German High Command, but no concrete evidence or locations have been given and it is thought that unsuspecting locations are still full of plundered goods including rich silk, Chinese rugs and ornate jewels. Yet it is not just artwork and artefacts that make up Hitler's collection; children's bathing suits, and thousands of pounds worth of Italian made garments, that could likely clothe the population of London for some years also exist. The collection is so extreme that the Regional Commissioner for Civil Affairs has appealed for more men, stating, *'Right now ... I could use five industrial officers, but above all send me a competent loot officer.'* It is not expected that the extraction and returning of the valuables to their rightful nations will be complete anytime soon, with inventories still needing to be carried out.

JUNE 4TH - 10TH 1945

IN THE NEWS

Monday 4   **"Mosquito's Make Record Time"** Britain to India in just over 12 hours is the headline that gripped the aviation industry as four of the RAF's Mosquito aircraft made the 4,600-mile trip from Britain to Karachi.

Tuesday 5   **"Broadcast Speeches"** The Prime Minister and the leader of the Labour Opposition have been allocated 10 broadcast speeches in the build-up to the General Election; it is believed the speeches have a large impact on how the electorate will vote.

Wednesday 6   **"Aluminium House on View"** The Government has commissioned over 50,000 new design aluminium houses. With streamlined manufacturing there should be a production of over 5,000 a month.

Thursday 7   **"Royal Welcome"** The King and Queen received a warm welcome when visiting the Channel Islands for the first time since they were liberated by Allied Forces. Jersey's Parliament met for the first time since before occupation in a triumphant service.

Friday 8   **"Getting Back to Civil Life"** Over 1,000 support centres have been opened across the country to accommodate the large number of resettled men and women forced from their homes during the war.

Saturday 9   **"Allied Commanders in Frankfort"** Marshal Zhukov flew to Frankfort-on-Main on his first visit to the territory occupied by the western allies where he bestowed the highest Russian Military honours on Field Marshall Montgomery and General Eisenhower.

Sunday 10   **"Civil Defence Farewell"** The King, Queen and Princess Elizabeth addressed a farewell parade in Hyde Park of representatives of the civil defence. The parade was headed by two rescue dogs who, on their trainers' command, barked as they passed the royal dais.

HERE IN BRITAIN
"Derby Day"

The sixth war-time Derby, on which £10m worth of bets were placed, was won by the favourite, Dante, in dominant fashion, and yet he was not the star of the show. Instead, equestrian news was filled with the record-breaking story of the '15 Guinea horse'.

The 100/1 outsider *Audentes* is undergoing a redemption story after being cast off and sold for just 15 Guineas at auction; his splayed feet, that caused much amusement at the auction, didn't hinder his performance however, as he came 18th out of the 27th runners.

AROUND THE WORLD
"Hitler's Body"

This week, *'responsible Russian officers'* in Berlin, stated that Hitler's body has been recovered and identified with 'fair certainty.' So long, however, as any shred of doubt exists, the Russians are loath to make an official statement. The charred body believed to be Hitler's, was one of four found in the fortress beneath the Reich chancellery, which had been burned beyond recognition by Russian flame-throwers. Russian doctors confirmed that he died from poison. The bodies of Goebbels and his wife and children, all of them killed by poisoning, were found in the same refuge.

D-DAY ANNIVERSARY

Supplies being uploaded whilst troops land in Normandy

The first anniversary of D-Day has seen elaborate celebrations across Normandy. After an official lunch for the French ministers of War, at Bayeux, there was a march past at the foot of the Arromanches cliffs, followed by a religious service to commemorate the British landing. The official party then attended a Franco-American military ceremony at Ste Marie du Mont before going to Ste Mere Eglise, the scene of some of the bitterest fighting after D Day.

In 1944, throughout the build-up to D-Day, General Eisenhower used several tactics and strategies to purposefully mislead the Nazi commanders into thinking the offensive was going to be staged at the Pas de Calais, rather than the Normandy beaches. Calais was the logical choice for such an attack, being the French point closest to mainland England, thus the deception did not require much convincing. Not only did Eisenhower 'leak' fake information through double agents, including a wild suggestion of Norway being a key landing spot, but also organised practical deceptions. A 'ghost army', under the command of George Patton, was sent to Calais together with a fake Mulberry Harbour, in such a way that it diverted attention away from the Normandy beaches, and many fraudulent radio-transmissions were planted. On the day, mine sweepers began to clear channels for the invasion fleet under cover of the bombing which began at midnight and finished just after dawn without encountering the enemy. Despite extensive planning and deception, the D-Day operation began far from smoothly. The day selected for the invasion, the 5th of July, was plagued with exceptionally rough seas, thus it was delayed by a further 24 hours, which increased the risk of German awareness. Nevertheless, the deception element of Operation Overlord proved to be an astounding success, with the Germans being unprepared for an invasion in Normandy.

JUNE 11TH - 17TH 1945

IN THE NEWS

Monday 11   **"200,000 Cars"** The motor industry is to produce a minimum of 200,000 private cars in the next 12 months. 40,000 are expected to be complete by the end of this year but during the first few months, deliveries will be on a limited scale as it is not possible to guarantee all necessary labour and materials.

Tuesday 12   **"Domestic Help in the Home"** *'The cornerstone of national life is at stake'* is just one report being used to justify the creation of a 'National Institute for Houseworkers'.

Wednesday 13   **"Farm Workers Needed"** The National Farmers' Union have lobbied the Government to release farm workers from service as an *'immediate priority'* to combat the expected loss of thousands of tons of food due to insufficient numbers of labourers.

Thursday 14   **"Russian Patriarchs in London"** Wearing golden robes and headdresses, a procession of Russian patriarchs was joined for the first time ever by the Archbishop of Canterbury, for a service in the Greek Orthodox Cathedral in London.

Friday 15   **"The Family Allowances Act"** Parliament has finally passed the Family Allowances Act granting financial support to families with multiple children. The Ministry of National Insurance will pay five shillings per week for every child other than the eldest.

Saturday 16   **"Doorless Houses"** Due to a shortage of timber, temporary houses from America as part of the lend-lease programme, are arriving without doors on cupboards or wardrobes.

Sunday 17   **"Home without the Wife"** Because of shipping limitations, the US Army has reported from its UK Headquarters that the British wives of US soldiers will not be able to travel to America for at least another 10 months.

HERE IN BRITAIN

"The Vexations of Peacetime"

Preparing for another period of austerity, the public thinks concessions should be made, and suggestions by readers of The Times include one lady, 'over seventy,' who writes, *'I believe the Government should give us rubber hot-water bottles before tyres for private motoring. Many old and ill people have suffered in winter from the lack of this comfort'.*

A Major from Berkshire wrote that his *'wife wants to know why the rubber face piece of a gas-mask - which must now be thrown away - cannot be used to provide hot-water bottles & suspenders.'*

AROUND THE WORLD

"Canadian Reparations"

A triumphant return of over 40,000 Canadian servicemen who fought for the Allies in Europe is in its provisional stages according to the Canadian Prime Minister. The preliminary plans would see all those servicemen who had been on the continent for over four years be drafted home, leaving approximately 35,000 men to continue occupational duties.

Injured men and liberated prisoners of war will take priority, followed by those with families in Canada. The plans involve Canadian naval vessels, but negotiations are ongoing with other United Nations powers about the possibility of air travel.

EISENHOWER - A LONDONER

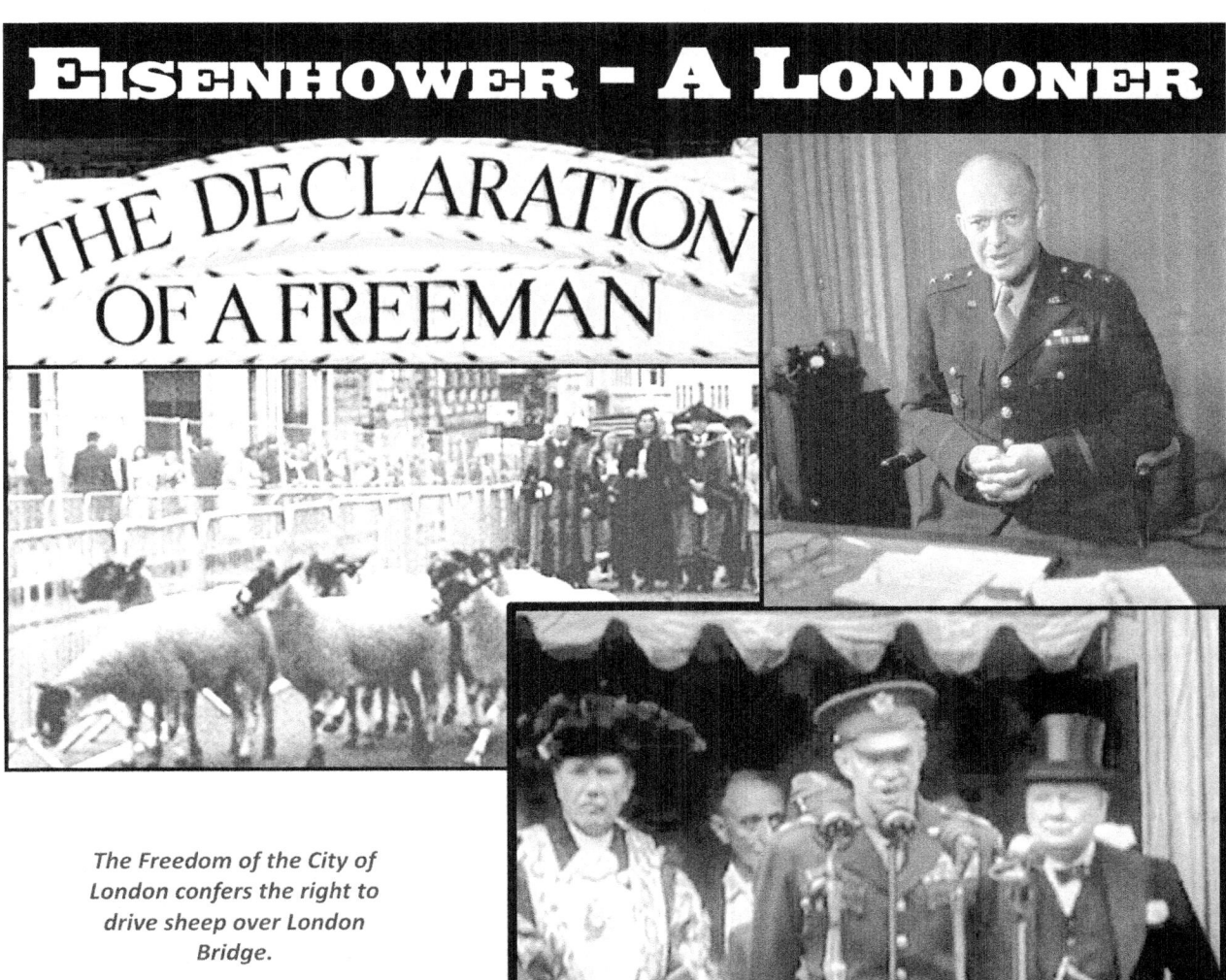

THE DECLARATION OF A FREEMAN

The Freedom of the City of London confers the right to drive sheep over London Bridge.

Large crowds lined the streets as General Eisenhower visited the Mansion House to receive his honorary 'Freedom of the City of London'. Having been entertained at lunch by Mr Churchill, a tribute was made to the General by the King at Buckingham Palace, when he conferred on him the Order of Merit. Eisenhower is the first American to be made a member of the Order, after it was bestowed on Marshal Foch and General Joffre after the First World War. Membership is limited to only 24. Cheers erupted from the crowd as Eisenhower began his speech from the Mansion House with *'whether or not you know it, I am now a Londoner myself ...'*

Freedom of the City was first recorded in 1237 and is closely tied to the role and status of the Livery Companies. It was, in earliest times, a requirement for all who wished to carry on business within the City. As a result, the privileges attached to the freemen were eagerly sought, while the duties and obligations were faithfully observed. It is still necessary to this day for all liverymen to be freemen of the City and it is the liverymen who elect the Lord Mayor and the Sheriffs of the Corporation of London. It is no longer necessary to be a freeman to work in the City, but from 1835, the freedom 'without the intervention of a Livery Company' could be purchased by nomination of two sponsors for a fee, known as a 'fine', of (now) £100, and is free to those on the electoral roll of the City. There are a number of rights traditionally but apocryphally associated with freemen including the right to drive sheep and cattle over London Bridge and carry a naked sword in public. However, these privileges are now effectively symbolic.

JUNE 18TH - 24TH 1945

IN THE NEWS

Monday 18   **"Demobilisation"** Plans for preliminary demobilisation of allied forces are to be implemented today after extensive planning. Ordered and sequential discharge by '*Classes*' are to begin with Class A men which includes those over 50, family men and former prisoners of war.

Tuesday 19   **"National Trust Jubilee"** At a lunch held to celebrate the jubilee of the National Trust, the Chairman announced the latest gift of Charlecote Park, near Stratford on Avon, which has many links to Shakespeare.

Wednesday 20   **"Reverse Lend-Lease"** The Queen Mary liner, still wearing her war-time grey paint, transported 14,000 American troops back to the US on her first voyage since VE day.

Thursday 21   **"Danish Eggs AND Butter"** For the first time since the war started, Danish eggs and butter landed at Hull. Over 240 tons of shell eggs and 650 tons of butter.

Friday 22   **"Society's Diamond Jubilee"** The Queen attended the diamond jubilee of the Society of Authors, Playwrights and Composers at Grosvenor House. Dr Masefield recited one of his own poems, '*Country Cure or the Boy who Swallowed a Frog.*'

Saturday 23   **"Britain's Aircraft Exhibition"** Opened on the bombed wreckage of John Lewis' Oxford Street, heavy rain prevented the flight by squadrons of RAF fighters, but large crowds gathered to cheer the contingents of airborne troops, including some of the men of Arnhem, who marched with bands to the site of the exhibition.

Sunday 24   **"Southend Trippers"** Trippers ventured to Southend in their sweltering thousands for the first seaside worthy day of the year; trains were packed, and many people were left behind. Temperatures were still at 23 degrees as the sun fell.

HERE IN BRITAIN
"Shortage of Wire Netting"

The War Department are burying large quantities of wire netting, perfect for the ongoing effort to repair damaged houses and for completing odd jobs. Although a permit is no longer required, the material is still scarce, begging the question of the War Ministry's motives. The Government reported that salvage officers are told to get rid of the '*unusable material*' in the most efficient way possible. The practice came to light after a man pleaded not guilty to stealing 6 yards of wire, which he had been ordered to dispose of by the War Office.

AROUND THE WORLD
"The Help Holland Fund"

Support for the *Help Holland Fund* was called for from the Mansion House following a downturn in donations over the last few months. The fund, created by the London Royal Exchange, was designed to support the Dutch, and this fresh request comes after the revelation that, the Germans, in addition to inflicting on the Dutch people the terrors of the Gestapo, slaying the Dutch leaders, tearing away from their homes 800,000 people, few of whom have yet returned, and flooding great parts of the country, had systematically looted machinery and household goods of every kind.

WATCHING THE ENEMY

The government has announced a new pay structure for the Royal Observer Corps, giving a substantial wage increase for the key contributors to the war effort who so often get overlooked. The Corps is nearly 30 years old, is some 40,000 strong, and has been doing a vital front-line job every second of the day and night since a week before the outbreak of the present war.

Briefly, their main task is to spot and plot the course of every aircraft, both hostile and friendly, which is over or approaching these shores. Throughout Britain there are 1,500 carefully sited observer posts, each manned every minute of the 24 hours by two highly trained observers. They are liable to have any one of nearly 300 types of friendly and hostile aircraft over their posts which are often situated in outlandish spots, on a hill or a headland, on top of a church tower or even on top of a tree in a pine wood.

They are manned day and night and the spotters 'tell' every outgoing or incoming aircraft by direct telephone line to the nearest ROC centre. Here there is a table like those used in Fighter operations rooms, on which the course of the aircraft is plotted. The centre keeps Fighter Command abreast of the situation and the RAF keeps a constant check on any developments. It is on information from the men and women of ROC that air raid warnings are sounded.

For security reasons the public have heard little of the ROC, they have not heard, for instance, of the countless lives which have been saved by ROC information on 'homing' crippled bombers returning from the Continent, nor of the many lives saved by alerting Air-Sea rescue to aircraft down in the sea.

JUNE 25TH - JULY 1ST 1945

IN THE NEWS

Monday 25 "Nomination Day" Today marked the nomination day for General Election candidates. Some 1,600 in total, 80 of them women, put their names forward for one of the 640 seats in Parliament.

Tuesday 26 "Foundations of the United Nations" The World Security Charter was signed unanimously at the San Francisco Conference by all 50 nations represented. Along with the Charter, approval for the statute of the International Court of Justice and the establishment of the Preparatory Commission received the green light.

Wednesday 27 "Election Campaigning" Support for the Prime Minister was shown throughout his first day's tour from Chequers through the heart of the industrial Midlands. His reception was so tumultuous and overwhelming that his programme was seriously delayed.

Thursday 28 "Centenary of St Mary's Hospital" The home of penicillin, St Mary's Hospital in Paddington, celebrated its 100th birthday since its foundation, with a concert in the Royal Albert Hall and a Lord Mayor's dinner at the Mansion House.

Friday 29 "Coach Tours Return" The Ministry of War Transport has permitted greater freedoms for private coach journeys, but they must still not exceed the pre-war 50-mile limit.

Saturday 30 "Lord Haw-Haw" William Joyce, otherwise known as 'Lord Haw Haw', was formally committed for trial under the 1931 Treason Act for broadcasting Nazi propaganda from Germany to Britain during the war. He opened broadcasts saying *'Germany calling, Germany calling'* in an upper-class English accent.

Sunday 1 July "Dominion Day" The observance of the day in London opened with a Canadian service of thanksgiving at Westminster Abbey attended by the King, Queen and Princess Elizabeth. Over 1,000 officers of the Dominion's three fighting forces were present.

HERE IN BRITAIN

"Glamour Curls"

According to a recent report by the Daily Mirror, 1 in 10 women between the ages of twenty and sixty purchase glamour curls to add to their hair … without their husbands or boyfriends knowing.

The report also stated that a further 1 in 10 women would buy them if raw materials were permitted to be brought over from Italy. During peacetime, Britain is one of the biggest exporters of hair, sending over 4,000 lbs per year to the USA, including 10 tons to Hollywood. Prices can reach up to £1 per ounce.

AROUND THE WORLD

"Ceremony of the Signature"

Delegates from the United Nations Conference queued up to add their signatures to the recently approved World Security Charter. The event in the Veterans Building started at 6am, and wasn't concluded until the mid-afternoon, with Lord Halifax representing the British signature. Against a backdrop of pale blue stood the flags of the 50 nations, and the documents lay upon a huge round table on which powerful lights played. Press cameras filmed the whole day and the scene, according to onlookers, resembled that of a Hollywood film set.

WHAT WOMEN WANT

Work in Woolwich on the 22 semi-detached Howard houses, the first group of post-war, permanent, prefabricated houses to be built for occupation, is well underway. However, it remains to be seen how many of the views of working housewives who were consulted by the Ministry on the 'Design of Dwellings', will be seen in practice. What women want most is privacy. They want enough room in their own homes to give privacy from the neighbours and privacy from family members too.

In country villages and towns, women are almost unanimous in wanting electricity and in rural areas where there is neither electricity nor gas, women want to by-pass the gas stage and go straight to electricity. By contrast, they do *not* want black lead, brass taps and dark, dust-collecting corners. A minimum of two sitting-rooms and three bedrooms is generally accepted for a family house and there is insistence on a hot water system, a minimum size of living room of 12ft by 15ft, adequate cupboard and storage accommodation, sound-proof walls and the suction method of refuse disposal. Working women's houses will have special wash houses where clothes could be dried and mangles.

These conclusions are based on the replies of more than 3,000 women from across England, to a list of questions prepared by the committee of Working Women's Organisations. '*The housewife,*' it states, '*looks at her house from three angles, the health of the family, the social centre for the family and her own work and leisure. She cannot be a good wife and mother unless she is also a good citizen, and for citizenship, she needs leisure from unnecessary drudgery*'. The planning of the house, the working equipment, materials, finishes and fittings are all be designed to save unnecessary toil.

JULY 2ND - 8TH 1945

IN THE NEWS

Monday 2   **"Austin to NYC"** A 10 horsepower, 4 door saloon Austin car is making its way to New York as part of a project by an American distributor who wants *'all the small British cars they can get"* to sell in the United States.

Tuesday 3   **"Shakespeare en France"** The Old Vic Theatre Company played Shakespeare's Richard III at the Comedie Française in Paris, becoming the first foreign group ever to be accorded the privilege. (The Germans played there during the occupation, but not by invitation.)

Wednesday 4   **"Royal Visit"** The King and Queen arrived at Douglas on the Isle of Man. Sirens wailed continuously as their boat came into view through the sea fog which all night had shrouded the coast.

Thursday 5   **"Polling Day"** Polling stations across the country opened their gates for the first General Election since 1935. Both the Conservatives and Labour are confident of victory.

Friday 6   **"Oil in the Thames"** An accident at the Oxford gasworks has contaminated the River Thames with oil for miles downstream. Swans could be seen clambering up the banks in attempts to escape, and many may have to be put down as they are covered in oil.

Saturday 7   **"High Quality Utility Clothing"** Higher quality utility clothing and their increased prices have been released by the Board of Trade. Men's ready-made suits will cost up to £8 12s and made-to-measure suits up to £10, compared with £5 7s. and £6 1s 3d.

Sunday 8   **"Sea Service Sunday"** King George's fund for sailors will benefit following a nationwide collection appeal entitled *'Sea Services Sunday'.* The money will be given to members of the Royal and Merchant Navy's.

HERE IN BRITAIN
"Dunlop's Contribution"

Exhibits from Dunlop factories are on display in London and most are from the previously *'secret list.'* Included are 100,000 different dinghies supplied to the Air Ministry, and thousands of barrage balloons, 4,000 of which were sent across the Atlantic after 'Pearl Harbour' to protect the Pacific coast of the US.

Another exhibit provides the answer to a mystery which long puzzled the Germans. On nights when no allied aircraft had been over the Reich, the inhabitants of many German towns found leaflets scattered on the ground. These were 'delivered' by Dunlop balloons.

AROUND THE WORLD
"The Show Goes On"

The Director of National Service Entertainment has stated that ENSA will continue to provide entertainment to all deployed servicemen until the end of the Pacific War. The news has been received well by all those still stationed abroad, who have been requesting further entertainment for some time now.

Orchestras, 250 solo musicians and four play companies will arrive in the Far East before the end of the year. Between 1939 and 1945, over 1 million performances were given to British and Commonwealth servicemen across the world, with audiences exceeding 300 million.

WAKES WEEKS

HOLIDAYMAKERS queue for trains at Blackburn Station in 1945

Rush to get away from the factory

Blackpool Promenade 1898

Voting in the general election was delayed for thousands of people in the north, as the date clashed with many of their annual holidays. The Lancashire 'Wakes Weeks' is a tradition that has been embedded in English culture for over half a millennium, having its roots in the late Medieval period. Originally a religious celebration, the week has since transformed into a secular holiday that supported the perceived beneficial properties of bathing in the sea during the summer months.

Throughout the Victorian era, during the Industrial Revolution and increased organisation of the factory industry, it became necessary to facilitate this week long break, with each Lancashire town designating a different week between July and September, as an unpaid holiday, whilst the mills and factories were closed for maintenance. It wasn't until 1906 that the unpaid holiday agreement was officially reached, which explicitly permitted 12 annual days holiday, including Bank Holidays, for all workers; the policy was implemented in 1907 and was increased to 15 days in 1915.

It was throughout the middle of the 19th Century that the Wakes Weeks truly burgeoned. With the increased accessibility of rail travel and a rapidly growing population moving to the towns to work in factories, more people had the opportunity to take 'days out' to the seaside. The railway link to Blackpool from the mill town of Oldham was completed in 1846 and in the peak year of 1860, more than 23,000 holidaymakers travelled on special trains to the resort during Wakes Week from that town alone. In the last quarter of the century, trips increased to full weeks away and 'Wakes Saving' or 'Going-Off' clubs, where workers paid a small amount each week so save up for their holiday, were a feature of the industrial north until paid annual leave was introduced in the 1940s.

JULY 9TH - 15TH 1945

IN THE NEWS

Monday 9   **"Putting up the Soldiers"** Hotels in seaside towns across the South of England are unable to take their usual quantity of holidaymakers this summer. The hotels and boarding houses are full with Australian and Canadian servicemen still unable to return home.

Tuesday 10   **"Mr Eden's Return"** The Foreign Minister, Sir Anthony Eden, has returned to the Foreign Office after almost two months away receiving treatment for a duodenal ulcer.

Wednesday 11   **"Milking It"** Milk allowance is set to reduce from three pints a week to two and a half now that milk production has passed its peak for the season. The change comes a fortnight later than last year.

Thursday 12   **"Yanks Go Home"** The Queen Mary led a fleet of American troopships containing 35,000 servicemen into New York Harbour in the second, and largest ever, movement of troops across the Atlantic.

Friday 13   **"The Tiergarten Ceremony"** Field Marshall Montgomery met with three senior Russian officers at the Brandenburg Gate, Berlin, where they were honoured with the Order of the British Empire in recognition of their efforts in holding off the Germans on the Eastern front.

Saturday 14   **"Clocks Go Back"** The two-hours period of summertime which began on April 2 came to an end when clocks were put back just one hour. This restored summertime to the normal one hour ahead of Greenwich mean time.

Sunday 15   **"London A Blaze"** Thousands of people witnessed a blaze of splendour, rather than the blazing fires the people of London had become so used to, across the Capital as streetlights were turned on for the first time in almost six years.

HERE IN BRITAIN

"Tanks in the New Forest"

The ancient Court of Verderers in Lyndhurst held a heated debate over whether the New Forest is to become the 'new Salisbury Plain', allowing the tank training proposed for the region. Residents spoke of the damage already done by tank operations in designated areas, leaving what was once luscious forest *an absolute desert.'*

The Army says Salisbury Plain is too small and they are looking for alternative training locations, but they are finding much resistance from residents. The agreement was originally that the army would leave following the end of the war.

AROUND THE WORLD

"Bastille Day"

An air of freedom in Paris dominated the celebrations in Paris for their first unoccupied Bastille Day since 1939. The clandestine celebrations of the previous years were made up for with three days of distinct celebration. Military processions during the day gave way to fireworks and bonfires at night, as the Parisian people celebrated their liberation from both last year, and some 150 years previously. Amongst the celebrations, the French military showcased a number of new weapons from America, which brought great cheers from crowds gathered for the event.

DOUBLE BRITISH SUMMER TIME

You can't stop time...

But you can turn it back one hour at 2am on July 15th when double daylight saving ends and standard summer time resumes.

The two-hours period of summer time which began on April 2 came to an end on Sunday 15th. Double British summertime, a policy implemented by the government since 1941 to increase sunlight which in turn helped to reduce the effects of blackout protocol stops. No longer will the clocks be two hours ahead of Greenwich Meantime, instead returning to their 1916 standard one hour ahead. First introduced in 1941, it was then used again for an extended two weeks in 1943, 1944 and finally, 1945.

British Summer Time was established by an act of parliament in 1916, following a campaign against the waste of working time on summer mornings. The practice involved putting clocks forward by one hour in Spring, so that mornings had one hour less daylight, and evenings one more. Clocks were then put back one hour on the last Sunday in October and summertime ended. The length of the actual day did not alter but sunrise and sunset appeared to be an hour later. From 1901-1936 King Edward VII operated a daylight-saving system at Sandringham because he loved hunting in winter. Therefore, all the clocks on the Norfolk estate were put forward by 30 minutes!

There have been many debates as to whether we should continue like this. In 1959 many wanted a permanent change to clocks going forward by one hour, and in 1966 the government introduced the British Standard Time Experiment, with clocks being one hour ahead all year before reverting to normal again. However, many farmers, as well as residents of Scotland and Northern Ireland, oppose doing away with British Summertime as it would mean that in parts, the winter sunrise would be at 10:00am or even later, and school children would travel in the dark, on colder, icier roads, possibly leading to more accidents.

JULY 16_{TH} - 22_{ND} 1945

IN THE NEWS

Monday 16   **"Radio Resumption"** The BBC's post war plan for home listeners to be implemented at the end of the month has been revealed. Two new programmes, named the Home Service and the Light Programme are being introduced which will run from 6:30am until midnight each day.

Tuesday 17   **"Magna Carta"** The British Museum has received the gift of the Lacock Abbey copy of Henry III's reissue of the Magna Carta from 1225. One of only two copies, the other residing in Durham, the document presents the Magna Carta in its final form.

Wednesday 18   **"Record House Build"** At 10am The Ministry of Aircraft Production delivered the first aluminium house to be erected for occupation to Shirehampton, Bristol. By 2:55pm, the house was built, furnished and ready to be inhabited.

Thursday 19   **"Petrol Rationing"** The Ministry of Fuel and Power has reported that it would be *'quite impractical'* to get rid of the current petrol rationing as the world supply of petrol is showing no signs of improving.

Friday 20   **"The Wallace Collection"** After nearly six years, the Wallace Art Collection has once again opened its doors, retaining all principal exhibits and 12 of its 22 pre-war galleries.

Saturday 21   **"50 Year Manchester Plan"** A 50-year plan was unveiled by Manchester City Council to create an image of what the city could look like in the future. Plans for a ring road and a revamped city centre has drawn the attention of large numbers of the public.

Sunday 22   **"Train Wreck"** An express train travelling between Glasgow and London was involved in an accident with a goods train resulting in 2 deaths and over 50 injuries. Over 100 passengers escaped.

HERE IN BRITAIN

"The 'New' Thing"

Steel, which made our modern civilisation, is now being overtaken by old fashioned wood for the production of car bodies, air planes, bicycles and even kitchen sinks.

Wood was the primary component in the Mosquito fighter plane and, according to the manager of the Metropolitan Plywood Co., a large number of car manufacturers have been in contact about supplies for the building of motorcars. Lighter and easier to repair and strengthen, moulded wooden frames are also planned for use in lightweight racing bicycles before the end of the year.

AROUND THE WORLD

"Halifax Lit Up"

A series of explosions lit up the city of Halifax in Canada, after a munitions factory some four miles from the city caught fire. The original explosion was felt for miles, destroying thousands of windows in homes and buildings across Halifax, reaching even the neighbouring city of Dartmouth. The fire was brought under control, and thankfully safely contained away from the hundreds of depth charges stored within the factory.

Over 17 thousand evacuated residents have been told to return to their homes after being setting up camps outside the city.

THE HALIFAX EXPLOSION

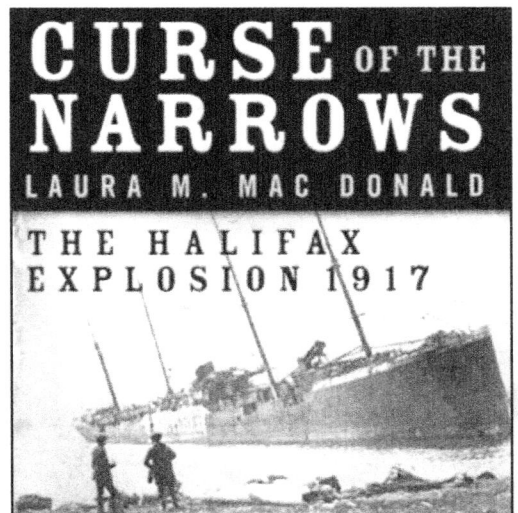

CURSE OF THE **NARROWS**

LAURA M. MAC DONALD

THE HALIFAX EXPLOSION 1917

The Boston Daily Globe

BOSTON, SATURDAY MORNING, DECEMBER 8, 1917—FOURTEEN PAGES

BLIZZARD CUTS OFF HALIFAX 20,000 SURVIVORS DESTITUTE

Trains Carrying Injured to Nearby Places For Treatment and Rushing Aid to Homeless Thousands Stalled in Deep Snow Drifts---
List of Dead May Reach 2800 With 3000 or More Hurt

Much of Halifax was flattened by the explosion

A munitions factory explosion some four miles out of the city rocked the Canadian port of Halifax as hundreds of tons of explosives went up in flames. However, this isn't the first time in the 20th Century that Halifax has been gripped by an explosive disaster. In 1917, the port was engulfed with flames when the Norwegian ship *Imo* crashed into a French munitions ship the *Mont Blanc* as it was leaving harbour. Halifax, Nova Scotia was the home of the Royal Canadian Navy during the First World War and became the key transport harbour between North America and Europe for the Royal Navy, shuttling men, coal, food and munitions across the Atlantic. Millions of supplies arrived in Halifax by train, to be shipped to Britain to help with the war effort, and a large number of Royal Navy vessels resided in the port, for refuelling, repairs or rest.

On 6th December, 1917, the two ships collided in the Narrows, the tightest part of the channel, after the *Imo* was forced to the wrong side of the river to avoid oncoming ships. The initial impact set the ships ablaze in a fire that burnt for over 20 minutes, sending billowing black smoke into the air, smoke which drew the people of Halifax and Dartmouth to their windows or the streets ... when the ship eventually did explode, the impact smashed windows across the city, blinding onlookers as shards of glass were sent like arrows into their faces, a gruesome and horrific image that has since been portrayed in *The Curse of the Narrows* by Laura M. MacDonald. Over 1,600 people were instantly killed, with a further 400 dying later from injury. The explosion damaged thousands of buildings and caused a tsunami, even smashing windows in Truro, over 100km away.

IN THE NEWS

Monday 23   **"Slums to Stay"** Local councils who have put in requests to demolish homes that are deemed to be unsafe have been denied permission from the Government, who are claiming *'a roof is a roof'* amidst the ongoing housing crisis.

Tuesday 24   **"Utility School Shoes"** Children are increasingly absent from school, often for weeks at a time, whilst their shoes are being repaired. The Board of Trade has been asked to help manufacture stronger children's shoes, able to withstand the normal 'wear and tear'.

Wednesday 25   **"Potato Rot"** Owing to port strikes in England, thousands of tons of potatoes are going to waste in Ireland as shipping quotas are not being fulfilled. Dockers say that the entire consignment of 1,000 tons accumulated for shipment by the Americans, has rotted.

Thursday 26   **"Sweeping Labour Victory"** In a landslide victory, Clement Attlee was triumphant in the General Election over war time Prime Minister Winston Churchill. Mr Churchill resigned this morning.

Friday 27   **"Cotton Recruitment"** The Cotton Board has embarked on a 'charm' campaign following the downturn in labour for Britain's premier industry; fully funded school trips to cotton mills are to be set up to show them the life is worthwhile.

Saturday 28   **"State Opening of Parliament"** The State Opening of Parliament has been delayed by a week to give Prime Minister Attlee, who has been in Germany at the Potsdam Conference, sufficient time to form a new Government.

Sunday 29   **"The Eighth Army Disbanded"** The Eighth Army, who saw war time action stretching between Cairo and the Austrian Alps, has been disbanded.

HERE IN BRITAIN

"The Port of London"

The war record of the greatest port in the world is shown in an exhibition of pictures, photographs, models, plus a German magnetic parachute mine weighing 2,700lb, with harness and parachute attached, which has been arranged in the bomb-scarred entrance hall of the Port of London Building.

Over the course of the war, some 100 million tons of goods passed through the port, which stretches between Teddington and the Nore lightship. The Thames was swept daily for mines from Kew to the sea and 1,000 Thames barges were used as landing craft.

AROUND THE WORLD

"Aga Kahn's Weight in Diamonds"

Followers of the Aga Kahn have opened an investment trust in East Africa with capital of £1 million. The Aga Kahn himself is putting up £250,000 in war bonds along with the proceeds of his upcoming diamond jubilee - his followers, who make up all the shareholders of the trust, have offered the Aga Kahn's own weight in diamonds to be added to the capital next year at nominal interest.

Whilst the trust's shareholders are all Ismailis, the investment banking and operations savings of the trust are open to the public.

MULBERRY HARBOURS

A view of Mulberry Harbour "B" at Arromanches, France in 1944.
The INSET shows how each module of the harbour is constructed before floating in to position.

As part of the London Port's exhibition, schoolchildren are being given talks about, and shown models of, the prefabricated 'Mulberry Harbours' used in the D-Day landing operations. The plans for artificial harbours stemmed from the calculation of the sheer numbers of resources required by the troops to maintain the invasion; the quantity needed was estimated to exceed 12 million tons, and the requirement of 2,500 vehicles. The planning for the D-Day operations began as early as summer 1943, therefore a solution to the problem needed to be worked out. Two artificial harbours were decided on, one for British and Canadian forces, named 'Mulberry B', and one for American troops, named 'Mulberry A'. The harbours were to be transported across the English Channel at the speed of 8kph by ships code named 'Corncobs', and deposited in 'Gooseberries', which was the nickname given to the sheltered water created by the Mulberry harbours.

The deployment of the harbours involved the sinking of concrete caissons, code named 'Phoenixes' to act as floating breakwaters; the structures weighed between 2,000 and 6,000 tons each and were sunk in the coastal waters just off the Kent shore prior to the offensive, having to be raised again and dragged across to Normandy, hence the name 'Phoenix'. Once in place, the Corncobs were then able to drag the Mulberries into place off the coast of Normandy, where Gooseberries were created, giving the forces ample still water for troop and supply deployment. 'Whales' were the names given to the landing piers, which were built out from the Normandy beaches.

The success of the Mulberry Harbours is a testament to the ingenuity of the combined British and American engineers and armed forces, successfully helping to provide supplies to the troops on the front line.

JULY 30TH - AUG 5TH 1945

IN THE NEWS

Monday 30   **"Channel Delays"** Nearly 4,000 troops have been held up in Calais on their way home to Britain for their scheduled leave, after rail strikes in London caused major congestion. Steamers in Calais were held back and leave for soldiers has been extended.

Tuesday 31   **"Soldiers in Surrey Docks"** Between 300 and 400 soldiers assisted with the unloading of ships at Surrey docks because of ongoing workers strikes. Almost two weeks have elapsed with no unloading taking place of ten of the eleven ships in the docks.

Wednesday 1   **"For-Never Amber"** The novel, *Forever Amber,* has been banned by the Australian Literacy Censorship Board for its *'blatant sexual references',* considering it not a desirable book for the people of Australia. The book has also been banned in 14 American states.

Thursday 2   **"Presidential Plymouth"** For the first time since the tenure of Woodrow Wilson, an American President will visit Britain, with President Truman arriving from the Potsdam Conference in Plymouth, where he will be entertained by the King.

Friday 3   **"Standard 8"** The Standard 8, an eight horsepower saloon car, which is now available for early delivery, is to cost £313 and be equipped with a sliding roof, two doors and a four-speed gearbox.

Saturday 4   **"Fishermen Strike"** The fish markets in Grimsby were left empty as British fishermen refused to take to the seas in protest against foreign fishermen landing their catches at the port, thereby reducing the local fishermen's income.

Sunday 5   **"Bank Holiday Weekend"** A good time was had by thousands over the country, but beer, breakfast and seating provisions were described as *'abominable'* in Brighton and Southend who handled the most visitors since the pre-war period.

HERE IN BRITAIN

"Nissen Huts"

Nissen huts no longer needed by the army are being sold by the Government for prices starting as low as £3. The huts, measuring 50ft by 16ft, are not suitable for living given their lack of sanitation provisions, but instead are being used and converted even into village dance halls. Farmers, who want them for agricultural storage, village institutions and bowling clubs are among those lining up to purchase the huts, of which hundreds were produced. The corrugated iron shells were mainly used in military barracks for storage and doubled as air raid shelters.

AROUND THE WORLD

"Blinded By Fog"

Air disaster struck in New York City as, blinded by fog and mist, a B-25 bomber crashed into the 79th floor of the Empire State Building. The impact happened at 900ft above sea level, killing 13 people including the three aboard the aircraft, in the crash and the fire which followed.

Luckily, the structural integrity of the building remains intact, but the damage done is estimated to cost £500,000. Because it was a Saturday in the summer, many of the building's 5,000 residents were out, and the number of 'transient' visitors less also.

FISHERMEN ON STRIKE

Grimsby trawlers being unloaded

Owners of Grimsby's 140 trawlers are trying to resolve their latest difficulty. With the North Sea and Atlantic free of German submarines and warships, fishermen from Iceland, Scandinavia and the Continent are now all at sea, fighting for the same fish. The Grimsby fishermen have gone on strike to try and get the authorities to limit or stop the foreign trawlers landing fish in their port.

With money and work hard to come by, the owners expect the strike soon to be over, but then they will face the more traditional problem of drunkenness. In the past they would put the offender in the long boat until he sobered up, but now they have brought in an expert to help. *"It must be remembered that the modern trawler costs £15,000 or more and the equipment on its bridge is becoming more highly technical. Our industry can no longer afford ridiculous accidents, either to the vessels or men."* In the meantime, when the trawler men return from three weeks or more at sea, they will receive a pamphlet spelling out the dangers of drunkenness. *"Although the days of the drunken, roughneck fisherman are long past"*, it reads, *"trouble is being caused by the small minority of men who think it is 'big' to get drunk before embarking on a trip."* Emphasising that drinkers constituted only a handful of men, and most skippers do not mind men taking a bottle of Scotch or something with them - as they are going off to sea for 21 to 24 days after only three days at home – it says there are still too many cases of men trying to swim ashore from ships and drowning; falling over the side; ending up in hospital badly injured – or being killed.

However, the last word comes from a disenchanted deckhand, *"You try fishing around the North Cape in bad weather. You need to be a bit drunk or a bit daft even to consider going to work in those conditions."*

Aug 6th – 12th 1945

IN THE NEWS

Monday 6   **"Doomsday"** The US Air Force have confirmed the dropping of the world's first nuclear bomb on the Japanese city of Hiroshima. Japanese news outlets reporting on the devastation cannot yet say the extent of the impact.

Tuesday 7   **"Stop the Strikes"** … *'and get on with the job'* was the plea to both workers and management at the opening of the Royal National Eisteddfod of Wales by the organisation's Vice-Chairman in his speech. The event has a record 17,000 entrants.

Wednesday 8   **"Postal Censorship"** Under a new Control of Communications Order, censorship permits are now required for shipments overseas **only** if they are going to China, Portugal, Spain, Sweden or Switzerland.

Thursday 9   **"Japanese Surrender"** Japan cowering under the Allies' devastating atomic bomb on Hiroshima and today on Nagasaki, her plight made yet more hopeless with the entry of Russia into the war, has accepted the Potsdam *'surrender or be destroyed'* ultimatum, bringing about the end of the war.

Friday 10   **"The Future of Women's Work"** A booklet by the Economic League shows how thousands of women, previously unskilled, became skilled tradeswomen during the war. It is aimed at potential employers, as women across the country are demobilised.

Saturday 11   **"The Best of British"** International demand for British books is once again growing throughout the countries of liberated Europe. Despite shortages of paper and transport, provisions are being made to resume commercial exports.

Sunday 12   **"Docks Go Slow"** Dockyard workers at Surrey Commercial Docks have decided not to resume work after two weeks of non-activity. The Union accounts for roughly 15% of the workforce in the port of London.

HERE IN BRITAIN

"Spontaneous Gaiety"

Despite explicit orders from the War Office that the news of the Japanese surrender should be treated with caution, servicemen and women across London erupted into spontaneous gaiety. Joining in celebrating what, to them, signified final victory, with the crowds lining the streets between Aldwych and Oxford Circus, forcing traffic to be diverted. People climbed lampposts shouting and waving Union Jack flags.

Although spirits were high, unrestrained celebrations are still reserved until an official announcement is made.

AROUND THE WORLD

"Free Passage"

An agreement has been reached between Britain and Australia which allows former British servicemen and women, along with their families, free passage to emigrate to the country. Australia wants, and needs, new, healthy citizens, and the policy is a continuation of the plan to bring across 50,000 British war orphans within three years. The Minister added that these plans would not be put into fruition until the return of all of Australia's deployed servicemen and an improvement in their ongoing housing crisis.

THE PROMENADE CONCERTS

Basil Cameron has assumed the reigns as conductor of this year's Proms following the death of Sir Henry Wood last year. Sir Henry was so integrated in the occasion that the Proms' official name became *The Henry Wood Promenade Concerts.* The works this year are as varied as ever, retaining ever popular acts but implementing new and modern performances alongside.

There have now been Promenade Concerts – literally, concerts where you can walk about, in London, for more than a hundred years and our present series can reasonably trace its ancestry to the entertainments in the public gardens of Vauxhall, Ranelagh and Marylebone in the eighteenth century. The original English promenade concerts at the Lyceum Theatre in 1838 were conducted by Musard and consisted of instrumental music of a light character, containing overtures, solos for a wind instrument and dance music (quadrilles and waltzes). The change from theatre to concert hall, Queen's Hall, was made by Robert Newman when, in 1895, he started the present series with Henry J Wood as conductor. Newman wished to generate a wider audience for concert hall music by offering low ticket prices and an informal atmosphere, where eating, drinking and smoking were allowed. He said, *"I am going to run nightly concerts and train the public by easy stages. Popular at first, gradually raising the standard until I have created a public for classical and modern music."*

In 1927, the BBC saw that taking the concerts on would provide a full season for broadcast and would fulfil the Corporation's remit to 'inform, educate and entertain'. After the Queen's Hall was bombed in 1941 the Proms moved to the Albert Hall where their policy remains, classics plus new works and among the established artists, promising newcomers.

AUG 13TH - 19TH 1945

IN THE NEWS

Monday 13   **"Not So 'Glorious Twelfth'"** August has begun with what has been hailed as the worst opening on record for grouse shooting in Scotland. In the Highlands few moors have been let and in some districts of Argyllshire there are practically no grouse owing to extensive burning of heather to clear the ground for grazing.

Tuesday 14   **"It's Official"** The Prime Minister, together with the Foreign Secretary Ernest Bevin, made a speech, broadcast to the nation from 10 Downing Street, officially announcing the Japanese surrender.

Wednesday 15 **"V-J Day"** Two days of national holiday to celebrate victory in Japan began today, with celebrations across the country marking the end of the Second World War.

Thursday 16   **"State Opening"** The State Opening of Parliament returned with full pomp and circumstance, with the King and Queen dressed in their ceremonial robes. The only change from pre-war tradition, was the location; the event was held in the House of Lords, as the House of Commons was damaged in enemy bombing raids.

Friday 17   **"More Petrol Ration"** The Ministry of Fuel and Power has announced that the basic petrol ration is to finally be increased, with hopes for further allowances in the coming months. The provision is going up from 120 to 150 miles.

Saturday 18   **"Mining Expectations"** Expectations of coal production has increased by nearly 250,000 tons per week following government plans for the nationalisation of the mines.

Sunday 19   **"National Day of Prayer and Thanksgiving"** The King, Queen and the two Princesses were present at St Paul's Cathedral where a special service honouring the British people took place. Countless other services took place all over the country.

HERE IN BRITAIN

"Contagious Happiness"

London was a city come alive, with people out on the streets celebrating the official end of the Second World War. Crowds flooded the streets and sounds of church-bells, whistles and fireworks drowned out the engines of cars and buses, honking their horns with elation. Even the heavy rain didn't dampen the spirit of the Londoners, some of whom camped outside Buckingham Palace just to catch a glimpse of the King and Queen on their way to St Paul's Cathedral. Vendors did a roaring trade, selling banners and streamers to passers-by.

AROUND THE WORLD

"Boots & Bicycle Weapons"

In Kasama, Northern Rhodesia, an African man was cycling to work and became aware that he was being followed by a lion. He put on speed and yelled, but the lion gained on him.

The man was wearing a heavy pair of military boots, which he managed to get off and throw at the lion giving him a moment's respite. But the lion came on again and was gaining on him, when the African jumped off and hurled his bicycle at the lion - who lost interest and turned back into the bush.

BEKONSCOT MODEL VILLAGE

The celebrations this week were not limited to V-J Day, the town of Bekonscot, Bucks, reached a landmark 500,000 visitors, all coming to admire the model kingdom of Lilliput, a beautiful micro-picture of quintessential English countryside which has drawn attention ever since its original conception in the late 1920s by Ronald Callingham and his gardener. The model was originally intended as a private miniature park, being formed after Callingham's wife prohibited him from enlarging his model railway inside the couple's house! Eager to continue his hobby, Callingham purchased four acres of land and relocated his railway; from there the project grew and grew, officially opening to the public in 1929, and by 1933, the village was open to visitors every Sunday between April and September.

Whilst the village is fictitious, a number of notable landmarks are dotted across the space, including train stations, libraries, a zoo and even a racecourse, all precisely measured to one inch to one foot scale, perfectly encapsulating 1930s England. An ongoing cricket match on the village green, men out for an afternoon on the golf course and children roughing it up in a boy scouts camp complete the list of fantastic additions to the village. 400 metres of railway represents over 10 miles in real life scale and the money raised from visitors has almost wholly been donated to charitable causes. By 1944, over £10,000 had been raised, creating such a buzz that even royalty came to visit, with the King, Queen and Princess Elizabeth attending on the Princess's eighth birthday.

IN THE NEWS

Monday 20 "Petrol Prices" Although plans have been released to cut the price of petrol by 2d to 1s 11½d a gallon (1p a litre), many motorists see this as *'putting the cart ahead of the horse'* as what people really want is a larger petrol allocation.

Tuesday 21 "The Loyal Addresses" The King and Queen drove to Westminster Abbey where they received loyal addresses from both Houses of Parliament. The ceremony, celebrating the return to international peace, took place in the Royal Gallery.

Wednesday 22 "Bevin's Boys Disappear" The Ministry of Labour has reported that many young mine workers have left their posts in recent months and are now unable to be found. The issue has been called *'a rather serious situation'* by a Ministry spokesperson.

Thursday 23 "Severn Bridge" Several million pounds are being put aside for the erection of the *'Severn Bridge'* so that work might start soon. Mechanical equipment released from aerodromes is expected to speed up the process.

Friday 24 "The Grim Facts" The Minister of Fuel and Power has released the *'grim facts'* that Britain would just about manage for fuel through the winter as long as everyone *'played the game'.*

Saturday 25 "British Army of the Rhine" Field Marshall Montgomery's 21st Army Group will cease to exist, instead being renamed the *'British Army of the Rhine (BAOR)'.* This now famous division is assuming its role as an occupying, rather than liberating force.

Sunday 26 "The Royals in Scotland" The King, Queen and two Princesses were greeted by hundreds of Scots when they arrived at Ballater station on their trip up to Balmoral Castle. The station was decorated with bunting and Pipers formed a guard of honour.

HERE IN BRITAIN

"Future of Floating Factories"

With a shortage on the European continent of oils and fats, the resumption of whaling has been made a priority by the Chamber of Shipping who will present their plans to the Ministries of Food, Agriculture and War Transport.

Among the products needed are whale meat, meat meal, and liver oil, rich in vitamin A. All 12 British whaling factories from before the war have been lost, and the report outlines the need for a further 20 floating factories, nine of which should be British, to average nearly 500,000 tons of whale oil a year.

AROUND THE WORLD

"German Coin Collection"

As part of a list of commands and prohibitions published this week, Germans in Soviet occupied zones must hand over all gold and silver currency and bars and all platinum bars; all foreign bank notes, coins, deeds, and valuables: all currency issued or prepared for issue in territory previously occupied by Germany or elsewhere now in possession of Germans to the offices of the State Bank. In addition, the wearing of German military uniform, or anything that resembles such is to be banned, and severe punishments for not abiding by these commands can be expected.

BARTLEMAS DAY

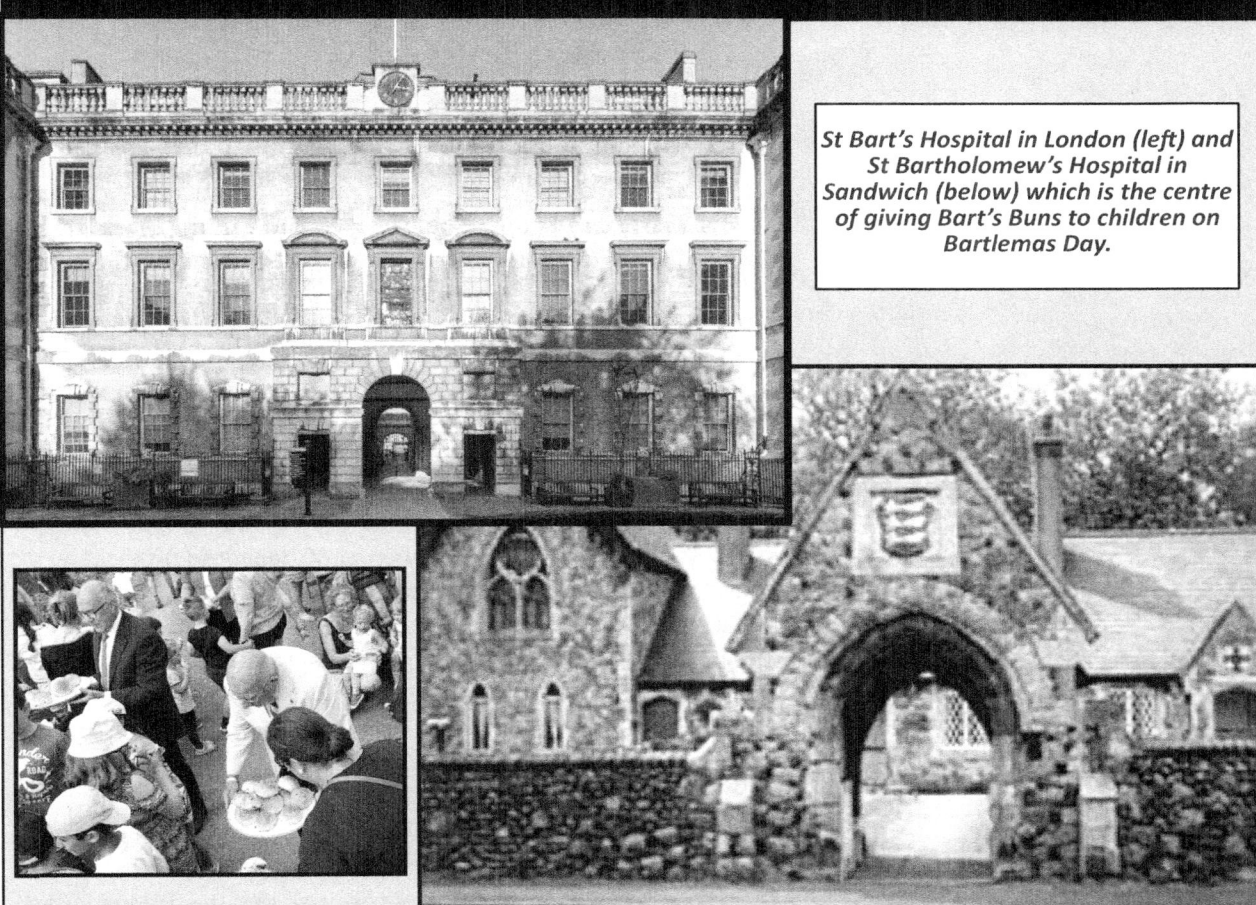

St Bart's Hospital in London (left) and St Bartholomew's Hospital in Sandwich (below) which is the centre of giving Bart's Buns to children on Bartlemas Day.

Saint Bartholomew was supposedly martyred by being flayed alive and this connection has made him the patron saint to butchers and tanners and by extension to bookbinders, for one of their traditional materials for binding books is leather. The Saint is best associated with two institutions, St Bart's Hospital in London and the ancient St Bartholomew's Fair. However, the Cinque Port of Sandwich in Kent also celebrates St Bartholomew's Day each August 24th. Among the most cherished institutions of the town is their St. Bartholomew's Hospital, not a traditional place for the sick, but a tranquil setting for the aged men and women of the town.

The records of the hospital give full details of its foundation in the reign of Richard the Lionheart, who landed at Sandwich on his return from the Crusades. There were four founding knights, and one of them, Sir Henry de Sandwich, has his tomb in the chapel of the hospital. These knights gave their land to provide a home for maimed mariners and the poor and elderly of the city to end their days in peace, and for more than 750 years, the 'brothers and sisters,' chosen by town worthies have lived on this same quiet site.

About 50 years ago the old hospital building of the middle ages was replaced by a quadrangle of little cottages, each standing in its garden with the ancient chapel, with its Norman arches, remaining in the centre. A service is held in the chapel on Bartlemas Day following which, the children of Sandwich run round the chapel and receive a current bun from the trustees of the hospital. The adults who attend the service are presented with a less edible 'St Bart's biscuit', a wafer stamped with the arms of Sandwich and the legend of the foundation.

IN THE NEWS

Monday 27 — **"Unsightly Advertising"** The CPRE is urging the government to protect rural areas from 'unsightly advertising.' They fear competition between businesses may result in many lovely places contaminated with signs.

Tuesday 28 — **"End of Lend Lease"** The Minister of Food is working hard to avoid imposing further food cuts following the conclusion of the US lend lease programme later this month.

Wednesday 29 — **"Meals from Down Under"** Because rabbits eat grass grown for sheep they are classed as a pest in New Zealand, so they are being shipped along with goat and hare to Britain to help with Britain's meat shortage.

Thursday 30 — **"Return to Hong Kong"** Crown forces triumphantly entered the Port of Hong Kong for the first time since December 1941. A fleet, some 30 vessels strong, delivered medical supplies for prisoners of war and troops thereby reinstating the port's trade.

Friday 31 — **"War Trials"** The trial of major war criminals is to begin in a joint venture between the United Kingdom, the Unites States, the Soviet Union and France.

Saturday 1 — **"War Gratuities"** Payment of war gratuities to the demobbed has begun and the Government is advising all men and women, honourably discharged from the armed forces, to apply.

Sunday 2 — **"Joy Cables"** The stream of free wireless calls, nicknamed 'joy cables', are coming in fast from liberated prisoners of war across Europe and the Far East back to England. The Edinburgh office of Cable and Wireless have people on hand day and night to make sure no calls are missed.

HERE IN BRITAIN

"Wanton and Vulgar Destruction"

Vandalism around the village and church of Imber in Wiltshire amounting to 'wanton and vulgar destruction' whilst troops were occupying and using the area for battle practice, is described in a letter sent by Lord Long to the Bishop of Salisbury. However, Long didn't stop there and is now seeking an inquiry from the War Office. Over £250,000 was invested in the village before the war, but now, cottage doors and windows had been deliberately smashed, and a fine staircase had been wrecked in the Court, a beautiful building restored in 1922.

AROUND THE WORLD

"Snails Big on Broadway"

Snail shell necklaces have taken Broadway by storm as 'society dames' strut down the famous streets wearing shells of all different colours. In England, in a hamlet in Wiltshire, seventy-four-year-old Goodwin Stubbs is out in the rain, among the hedgerows, collecting more snail shells, making the necklaces by hand to ship to America. The craze began after he gave his creations to some GI's stationed nearby who took them across the Atlantic. Mr Stubbs spoke of Americans offering him large sums of money to expedite their orders, but 'they must wait their turn'.

Former Prime Minister Winston Churchill has refused to accept the honour of The Order of the Garter bestowed on him by the King. The war time Prime Minister, whilst honoured to have been awarded the Order, explained that '*I can hardly accept the Order of the Garter from the king after the people have given me the Order of the Boot.*'

The Order is dedicated to Saint George, patron saint of England and appointments are typically made in recognition of national contribution, or service to the Crown. Membership of the order is limited to the sovereign, the heir to the throne and no more than 24 living members, or Companions. Churchill would have been one of only four 'commoners' to have ever been awarded the Order, and it is only in recent times that the infrequent appointment of regular folk has been somewhat normalised.

After defeating the French at the Battle of Crecy King Edward III founded a College of St George at Windsor in 1348 – a community of priests and 24 knights, each provided with a stall in the chapel. In 1942, because of their hostilities during World War II, Emperor Hirohito of Japan was struck off the list of Garter knights and the Japanese imperial banner was removed from St George's Chapel.

Appointments are announced on 23rd April, which is St George's Day, and Garter Day takes place in June. After the Investiture ceremony, lunch is served in the Waterloo Chamber and then the procession makes its way to St George's Chapel for a service, accompanied by the Heralds and the Yeomen of the Guard all wearing full ceremonial robes and uniform. The public crowd into the streets of Windsor to see this historic spectacle, one of the major events in the 'royal watcher's' calendar each year.

SEPT 3RD - 9TH 1945

IN THE NEWS

Monday 3   **"Forces Families"** Flags were being sold across London in celebration of the 'Forces and Forces Families Day' to help raise money for ex-servicemen during the resettlement period. It is hoped that donations will come from people recently returned to London.

Tuesday 4   **"Stamping it Out"** Pale wartime postage stamps are gradually to be phased out and be replaced by the darker, fresher pre-war versions. The change was made in 1941 to preserve dwindling dye supplies.

Wednesday 5   **"Mothers in Line"** The long queues at shops across the country since the beginning of the year has stirred the Minister for Food to propose a new scheme allowing expectant mothers to be given priority position. The women would have to possess a *'Queue priority, please'* red label.

Thursday 6   **"The Envy of All Countries"** The Minister for Health has stated that he plans to equip the country with a new nationalised health system that will be *'the envy of all countries'* but not until after the current housing crisis is resolved.

Friday 7   **"Trans-Atlantic Record"** The record time for the journey across the Atlantic Ocean by plane has been emphatically won by an RAF Mosquito; the plane did the crossing in just seven hours and two minutes in sub-optimal conditions.

Saturday 8   **"The New Governors"** Both Northern Ireland and the Isle of Man have sworn in new Governors. The exchanges took place face to face, breaking the age-old tradition that the outgoing and incoming officials should not meet.

Sunday 9   **"Hong Kong Jubilation"** Camp Stanley in Hong Kong was the scene of joyful celebrations and singing of the national anthem as the Union Jack was hoisted above the base for the first time in over three years.

HERE IN BRITAIN

"Mobile Medicine Exhibition"

A mobile exhibition has begun its tour of the West Country exhibiting the medical advancements made during the war. Organised by St Mary's Hospital, penicillin and DDT are highlights and there is a useful guide to the choice of balanced diets in these days of austerity feeding. Stark images of before and after war wounds treated by new techniques are somewhat gruesome and visitor discretion is advised. The exhibition is set to raise funds for the equipment needed for the proposed National Health Service.

AROUND THE WORLD

"From War to Peace"

The United States Director of War Mobilisation and Reconversion has disclosed the country's plans for the conversion from *'war to peace'*. In an ambitious plan, the Director proposed the demobilisation of over 8.8 million people in just under 8 months, with the removal of price restrictions and the suggestion of a 48-hour working week. It is clear that the stability of the economy is the top priority, as restrictions on petrol, fuel oil, oil cooking and heating stoves, and processed foods were removed less than 24 hours after the Japanese surrender.

WAR GRAVES COMMISSION

The restoration, where necessary, of the thousands of war graves in cemeteries and memorials across France and Belgium from the First World War is underway. The Imperial War Graves Commission (Commonwealth War Graves Commission since 1960) was originally set up to erect and maintain the war graves of Commonwealth soldiers who died between 1914 and 1918. Fabian Ware, after being told he was too old to join the British Army in 1914, became the commander of a mobile unit of the Red Cross serving on the front line in France, September 1914. He was struck by how little recognition there was for those killed, let alone marking of their graves, and as such he set up an organisation within the Red Cross for that very purpose. Ware established the Graves Registration Commission and received official recognition from the War Office in 1915. By May 1916, the Commission had over 50,000 registered graves in France and Belgium alone.

After negotiating with the French Government, Ware managed to establish grave registration sites where cemeteries would be made, and maintained, by the British; as news of this work became public across the then Empire, the Commission was flooded with letters asking for photos of the graves from relatives and by 1917, over 17,000 pictures had been sent home. By 1918, there were over 587,000 identified graves, but there were still 559,000 fatalities with no known grave. Now constituting six member states, the Commission has over 23,000 locations across 150 different countries.

IN THE NEWS

Monday 10   **"Norwegian Traitor"** Vidkun Quisling, the first Norwegian traitor has been found guilty of high treason and sentenced to death for offences against the military criminal law, the civil criminal law, and the regulations made by the Norwegian Government in London.

Tuesday 11   **"Coffee Ration"** Coffee lovers were the only people who could find comfort in the statements from the Ministry of Food, where it was announced that coffee allocation would increase by a fifth. This is possible because of the reduction in demands from the services and recent purchases from Brazil and Colombia.

Wednesday 12   **"WVS to Continue"** The Women's Voluntary Service will have a continued role during the transitional post war period, with added responsibilities. The WVS for Civil Defence, as it is known currently, will soon drop the *Civil Defence* from its title.

Thursday 13   **"House Rush"** Over 500 people queued outside the National Housing Trust offices in Birmingham, as they unveiled 400 leasehold houses costing from £500 to £575.

Friday 14   **"Belfast's New Freeman"** Field Marshall Montgomery was given a spirited Irish welcome as he arrived in Belfast to accept the Freedom of the City. Testaments flooded into City Hall, full of Irish and Imperial patriotism.

Saturday 15   **"Attention to Attlee"** The Prime Minister, Clement Attlee, spoke in Trafalgar Square to mark the London Thanksgivings Week opening ceremony; the event is the fifth since the beginning of the war and has the highest ever target of £125 million to be raised.

Sunday 16   **"Battle of Britain Thanksgiving"** The fifth anniversary of the Battle of Britain, marked yesterday, prompted a special service of Thanksgiving at Westminster Abbey, with a demonstration flight passing over the city by RAF Fighter Command.

HERE IN BRITAIN

"Stocks of Stockings"

Free pairs of nylon stockings will be available for girls across the country in a new scheme announced by British manufacturers. Over 18,000 pairs are ready to be given to some 2,000 women, who will all receive half a dozen sets each, one for each working day.

The lucky girls are all employees of six British hosiery firms who have been experimenting with nylon yarn, and the women are expected to provide feedback on comfort and utility. The nylon yarn, formerly used for war purposes, is hopefully soon to be widespread.

AROUND THE WORLD

"Gifts of Surrender"

The war on the Solomon Islands has finally ended with the signing of six pieces of paper in Bougainville this week. Commanders of the Japanese Seventeenth army brought gifts for the Australian Army Corps Lieutenant General.

The gifts included two ornate 'willow pattern' blue vases; some 12 inches tall. After opening the treasure chests they arrived in, from a safe distance, the surrender treaty was signed. The Japanese commanders explained how the gifts were homage to the Australian men killed.

NATION'S HOMAGE TO RAF

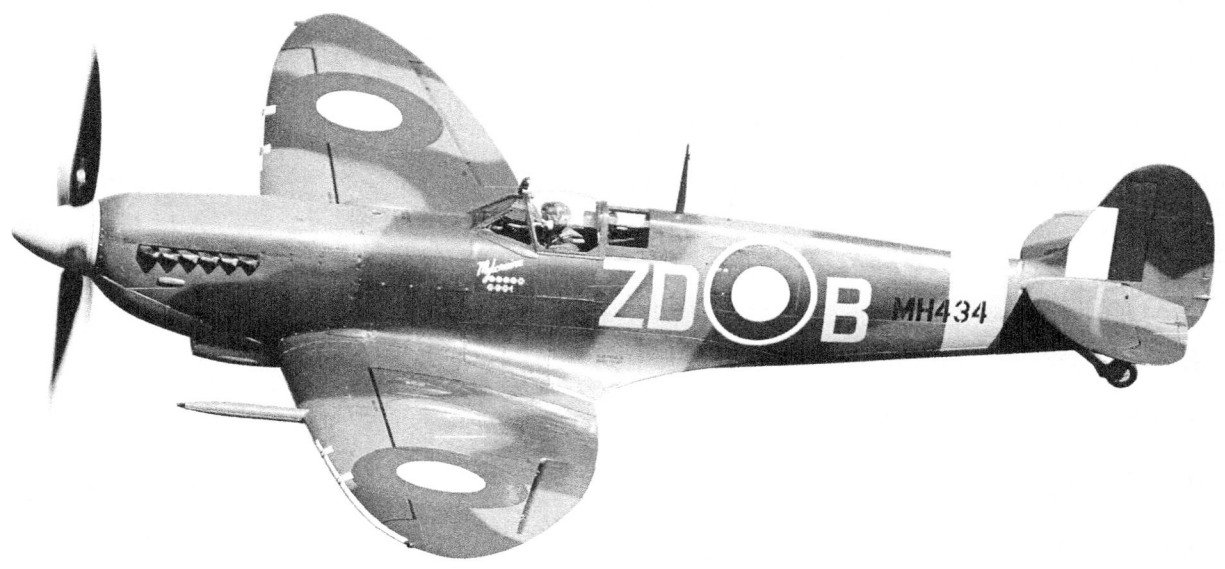

The RAF Spitfire

On Battle of Britain Sunday, all over the country, in places of worship, on village greens, at Royal Air Force stations and service camps, the people of Britain gathered to give thanks for victory, and to remember the sacrifice of those who died.

The RAF was formed at a critical period of the last war, by the amalgamation of the Army's and Navy's flying wings, the Royal Flying Corps and the Royal Naval Air Service. It came into being after three years and eight months of war. When the war of 1914 started, the aeroplane was a new and untried weapon, strictly limited in its uses and not sure of its role. Rapidly it developed both as a weapon of offence and defence. When the allies mounted their counter-offensive in 1918, the RAF was able to concentrate 1,290 first-line aircraft against its opponents' 340, and, enjoying this air superiority, was able to disrupt the Germans' communications and harass their troops by low flying attacks. When the Armistice came, the RAF was the greatest air force in the world, both numerically and in quality of equipment, possessing more than 200 squadrons, 22,647 aircraft of all, 103 airships and a total strength of 291,000 officers and men. After the war the Service shrank to a shadow of its former self but managed to keep many members possessing a pioneering spirit, which in turn, maintained the high standards and increased the prestige of British aviation throughout the world.

At the beginning of this war, we had far fewer planes than Germany and the country has undergone a massive drive to build Spitfires and Hurricane fighters, and Wellington, Whitley and Hampden bombers. All technically superior to the German planes, but it was, nonetheless, a dangerous situation until the Battle of Britain had been won.

IN THE NEWS

Monday 17   **"Fighting Services Day"** The celebrations for London's Thanksgiving week culminated in a march from the City to Trafalgar Square by servicemen from all three armed forces; the group were cheered on by workers and holidaymakers alike.

Tuesday 18   **"Faroe Gunpowder Plot"** An attempt was made in the early hours of the morning to blow up the Faroe Island's Parliament building, by disaffected nationalists, opposed to Danish rule. Although the explosion was violent, little major damage was done.

Wednesday 19   **"Lord Haw-Haw-no-more"** The trial of William Joyce, otherwise known as Lord Haw-Haw, has concluded with the defendant being convicted of high treason and thus sentenced to death by hanging. Joyce was found guilty of transmitting German propaganda.

Thursday 20   **"Return of the Restaurant Car"** The Minister of Transport has announced the return of the restaurant car on 84 trains across 42 different lines from October. The plans however are dependent on staff being available.

Friday 21   **"Orange Shipments"** Thousands of tons of oranges and jam are being crammed into the holds and decks of regular cargo ships in South Africa ready to be transported to Britain and the rest of Europe. There is an acute shortage of refrigerator ships.

Saturday 22   **"The All-New Morris Eight"** The cheapest post war British car yet, the first ever Morris Eight has rolled off the production line. For as little as £235 the two-door saloon version could be yours, including a free spare tyre.

Sunday 23   **"Vickers Viking"** Orders for the Vickers Viking twin-engine airliner have been placed by the British Overseas Airways and the RAF Transport Command. With a top speed of 252mph, the aircraft will be mass produced, culminating in 25-30 units per month.

HERE IN BRITAIN

"Wastepaper Recovery"

Save your paper is the message being heralded by the Wastepaper Recovery Association, at their exhibition in Hyde Park containing examples of the many different uses for re-purposed paper. The exhibit showcases plasterboard, linings for houses and factories, cable insulation, engine gaskets and petrol tanks all made from recycled paper. The aim is to raise awareness of the continued need to recycle paper in peace time, as we did during the war. *"It would be a scandal"* to have to purchase items that could so easily be created.

AROUND THE WORLD

"Golden Cruise"

It has been revealed that two of the largest ever consignments of gold to travel by sea were shipped from South Africa to the United States in the early years of the war. The gold, valued at over £30 million, was transported in two shipments during the height of the Battle of Britain and when U-Boats were at their most prevalent.

After being moved from Capetown to Simonstown under the cover of darkness, the gold was loaded onto a fast cruiser which made the journey to New York in record time.

ADMIRALTY DIVING UNIT

Landing Craft Obstruction Clearance Unit.		
No.	Rank or Rating.	Duty.
1	Lieutenant or Sub-Lieutenant ...	Commanding Officer
1	P.O.	——
2	Leading Seamen	——
13	A.B. or Ordinary Seamen (includes 1 S.D.).	——
1	Signalman or Ordinary Signalman	——
Total	1 officer	
	17 ratings	

Members of the Admiralty Experimental Diving Unit (ADEU) were at the Kingston baths in Surrey, where they demonstrated how a specially trained force successfully cut away underwater obstacles of the 'Atlantic Wall' to facilitate the D-Day landings in 1944. A combination of men from the ADEU, the Landing Craft Obstruction Clearance Unit and midget submarine crews took part in the demonstration exercise, of what has been called one of the most dangerous operations of the entire war.

During the actual mission, some 120 Royal Marines and Navy troops crossed the channel several hours before dawn, before transferring to small dinghies which they were forced to paddle to avoid noise detection. Equipped with 90 minutes' worth of oxygen, the teams dived to assess the level of underwater fortification. 10ft by 10ft steel barricades, 5ft high metal pyramids, pointed steel 'hedgehogs' and underwater mines were just some of the challenges encountered but nevertheless, by nightfall that same day, over 2,400 obstacles had been cleared, leaving a free space of over 1,000 yards. Clearance was done using explosive charges, which were swum from the dinghies with fish like efficiency; it wasn't enough to merely blow up the fortifications, as it required exact calculations to not leave any obstacle which could still be a danger.

For the Kingston demonstration, wooden poles represented obstacles, and the 'frogmen' as they had been named, were not working from dawn until dusk. Nevertheless, the enormity of the endeavour was made apparent, and the ADEU thanked Dunlop for their superior British underwater suits, especially compared to those of the Germans and Italians. The division has been active since 1933, designed to combat issues of port clearance; although its staff were largely made up from naval personnel and scientists, the unit was only militarised during the Second World War.

SEPT 24TH - 30TH 1945

IN THE NEWS

Monday 24   **"£200 A Second"** London raised a staggering £140 million during its Thanksgiving week savings effort, which equates to £200 donated per second.

Tuesday 25   **"Bluecoat Boys in the City"** The boys of Christ's Hospital Horsham visited London, for the first time since 1938, and marched to the Mansion House for the traditional reception by the Lord Mayor and the St Matthew's day service. Gifts of money were distributed to the 300 boys by the Lord Mayor.

Wednesday 26   **"No More Free Forces Fishing"** The scheme that for six years provided members of the British armed forces with free facilities for salmon and sea trout fishing, is concluding at the end of the month.

Thursday 27   **"Night-Time Speed Limit"** A 20mph speed limit will no longer be enforced in urban areas during times of darkness now that streetlamps across the country are back on. A uniform 30mph in towns and cities will now be in force for 24 hours a day.

Friday 28   **"The King's Fleet"** The King and Queen, accompanied by the Princesses Elizabeth and Margaret, paid a visit to the Home Fleet on their way back from Edinburgh.

Saturday 29   **"Long Socks … Not For You"** The long sock trade in Britain is to resume, but with 100% of all products being shipped abroad. There is no indication that the Board of Trade will allow the internal sale of long socks in the foreseeable future.

Sunday 30   **"School Leaving Age"** No attempt will be made to postpone the raising of the minimum leaving age for school students to 15, beyond April 1947. The change will affect around 339,000 children across the country.

HERE IN BRITAIN

"Ladybower Reservoir"

In a special ceremony organised by the Derwent Valley Water Board, the King unlocked the massive wrought iron gates to signify that the new £6 million Ladybower Reservoir was now officially opened. Three memorial tablets attached to an obelisk were unveiled by His Majesty, before he placed a copper cylinder containing various memorabilia beneath one of the large stone blocks forming the spillway. Current coins, a copy of the Times announcing the opening of the Reservoir, and the V-Day edition of the London News now sit at the bottom of the lake.

AROUND THE WORLD

"New York Lift Strike"

15,000 lift operators show no sign of letting up with their strikes across many of the high-rise buildings in Manhattan. The strikes are inconveniencing hundreds of thousands of people and there is no sign of an agreement being reached. Instead, threats of expansion across all five of the city's districts are being proposed which would affect many more lofty apartments and office buildings, in some cases, blocks exceeding 20 storeys, which will undoubtedly cripple the city's business districts. Even the hotel lift men are contemplating coming 'out in sympathy'.

MICHAELMAS DAY

Nottingham Goose Fair (main). A goose market (inset).

The Feast of Michael and All Angels Day, known as Michaelmas, was celebrated on the 29th September with religious ceremonies up and down the country. The day traditionally marks the beginning of Autumn and the official shortening of days, marking one of the four 'quarter days' in England. *Lady Day* in March, *Midsummer* in June, *Michaelmas* in September and *Christmas* in December make up the four 'quarter days' in traditional British folklore; spaced three months apart, the days all typically hold religious meaning and fall near an equinox or a solstice. It was on these days that servants were hired or fired, rent was collected and leases were signed. Michaelmas was originally particularly important, as it marked the end of the harvest season, but this became less so following the split from the Catholic Church under Henry VIII in the early 1530s, when the *Harvest Festival* was celebrated a few weeks later on October 10th.

Thousands of families across Britain feasted on a well fattened goose to, according to tradition, protect against financial need in the family for the next year: '*Eat a goose on Michaelmas Day, want not for money all the year.*' Because of this, Michaelmas has earned the nickname '*Goose Day*' and the famous Nottingham Goose fair is still held on the weekend closest to the festival. It stems from a rumour that goose was the food being eaten by Queen Elizabeth I upon hearing of the defeat of the Spanish Armada in 1588, vowing to finish the bird on Michaelmas in celebration.

In British folklore, Michaelmas is the last time that blackberries should be picked, as it was on this day that Lucifer was expelled from heaven, landing on a prickly blackberry bush, and proceeding to scorch it with fiery breath.

OCT 1ST – OCT 7TH 1945

IN THE NEWS

Monday 1   **"Exit Permits Abolished"** After six long years, exit permits will no longer be required for British citizens leaving the country. However, due to the large reliance on manpower, restrictions will remain for men over the age of 18 who are still liable for national service.

Tuesday 2   **"Af-ford-able Motoring"** The Dorchester Hotel in London was the site for the exhibition of two new British-built Ford motorcars. The sales manager announced the updated Anglia and Prefect whilst boasting they are the cheapest post war production car on sale.

Wednesday 3   **"Mersey Docks Strike"** Over 15,000 men were on strike at Mersey Docks leaving the shipyard idle. The strikes have caused problems to vessels in the Channel, with 48 deep-sea ships and a further 40 coastal boats affected.

Thursday 4   **"Pedestrian Must-Crossings"** New plans drawn up by the Government will give powers to the Ministry of Transport to compel pedestrians to cross at designated crossings; the public will be 'guided' to spots by fences.

Friday 5   **"Changing of the Guard"** The ancient ceremony of the Changing of the Guard was resumed for the first time since before the war. Contrary to the pre-war glittering breastplates and scarlet tunics, the Guards instead will wear their khaki service dress.

Saturday 6   **"Shoe Shortage"** Even though the production of children's shoes increased by over 300% during the war, there is still a large deficit, and many parents are left unable to purchase footwear for their children.

Sunday 7   **"Return from Afar-east"** The first cohort of liberated prisoners of war from the Far East have returned to Britain via Southampton Port; each man received a copy of a 'Royal Welcome Home' endowed with the King's signature.

HERE IN BRITAIN

"Going to the Dogs"

Birmingham City Council has banned dog racing meets on Fridays, or rather, payday. The President of the National Saving's Committee made the announcement this week, deploring the excessive betting on dog racing and its negative effect on the city community. He spoke of the Committee's experience of seeing men who had lost the entirety of their savings, and it is hoped that the policy will help to prevent such irresponsible expenditure by limiting the funds at participants' disposal. In the last 6 months, over £3.5 million has been placed on dog races.

AROUND THE WORLD

"California Burning "

In the last week over 800 acres of land across California have been devastated as the state faces its worst fires on record. Blazes from the Mexican border all the way to South Los Angeles have ravaged homes and displaced thousands of people.

Vital naval and marine bases near San Diego have been hit hard, causing major military disruption and further chaos as the fires are even affecting the city itself. A huge plume of smoke, visible from the air, covers the area and ashes drop like snowflakes from the sky.

HOME FROM THE EAST

The P & O Corfu (main). PoWs arrive on the Corfu in Southampton (inset).

The first ship bringing prisoners of war from the Far East arrived at Southampton to a warm welcome from friends and family gathered ashore. The P&O liner Corfu shipped over 1,000 troops to Britain, many of whom could be seen shedding tears as they disembarked to a sea of cheers. A message from the King and Queen was read out, speaking of the suffering endured and the courage of the men, before each soldier received an individual copy, typed on Buckingham Palace notepaper and bearing the King's signature.

The Corfu made good time on her voyage from Singapore and although looking largely well, the toll of the Japanese camps was evident on the faces and bodies of many. *'It was so bad that I wish to forget it'* said one soldier, and it soon became clear that the men were unwilling to discuss what went on during their captivity. The Changi jail in Singapore was home to one of the largest cohorts of British POWs in the Far East during the war and is notorious for its torturous conditions; some of the men had been captive for three and a half years, in the prison and neighbouring barracks, in which the Japanese military detained some 3,000 civilians and 50,000 allied servicemen.

Representatives from the Red Cross and St John's were waiting for the ship, and from mobile canteens, workers handed out gifts of chocolate and cigarettes to the servicemen. The highlight of the day however, although this story cannot be verified, was undoubtedly one man's defiance of the quarantine regulations, bringing delight to onlookers as he was followed off the ship by a duck, all the way from Rangoon. It is said that the duck then lay an egg on the quayside, and in doing so, cemented itself as a firm favourite.

OCT 8TH - 14TH 1945

IN THE NEWS

Monday 8   **"Troops to Unload"** Because of ongoing strikes at major ports across Britain, servicemen and women are being used to help with the unloading of ships to prevent a national food emergency. The present stoppage of work is of serious concern to the Ministry of Food.

Tuesday 9   **"Armistice Day as Usual"** The King has announced that Armistice Day will go ahead in its pre-war format, not only remembering those who fought in the Great War of 1914-1918, but also now, the most recent conflict.

Wednesday 10 **"London Without an Airport"** With three American airline services to begin regular flights from North America to Europe, London finds itself still without a practical commercial airport. Heath Row, the proposed terminal on the Bath Road, will not be completed for at least 18 months.

Thursday 11   **"Southampton Won't Strike"** Whilst declaring sympathy for the 30,000 dockworkers on strike at other ports, Southampton Dock's Union leaders don't want to '*take action which would give the enemies of the working class every chance to disrupt their organisation and bring into discredit the Government they helped to elect*'.

Friday 12   **"Newspapers to Stay Small"** The Government ruling to increase the size of newspapers has been indefinitely postponed because of the continued shortage of the necessary newsprint which is almost entirely imported from Canada.

Saturday 13   **"Royal Academy War Exhibition"** The Royal Academy has unveiled its new war exhibition, available to the general public. Starting from 1940, the exhibition showcases all aspects of the war on the land, sea and in the air.

Sunday 14   **"Interim Slum Repairs"** The Government has unveiled a 10-year housing programme reflecting the dire need for slum repairs in areas marked for redevelopment.

HERE IN BRITAIN

"Citizen's Advice Bureau"

The Citizen's Advice Bureau, responsible for over 170,000 inquiries a month, is to remain in place following the continued post-war demand. Originally designed as a war time service, the Bureau's enduring public use and lack of a parallel anywhere else in the world, has led to the decision to retain it as a civilian support network. Rehousing settlements have been reported as the most common enquiry, in spite of over 370 resettlement advice offices being opened by the Government in the last year. Close participation between the Bureau and the Government is expected.

AROUND THE WORLD

"Soldier's Wives Stuck"

The transport of British and European wives of US soldiers to North America may be delayed indefinitely following an announcement by the US Military Operational HQ in Europe. Due to the return of troop transport ships back to the British navy in exchange for continued use of the Queen Mary, the return of US servicemen home has significantly slowed, with a further 125,000 still needing transport over the next three months. Priority on British vessels are Canadian servicemen, who will begin repatriation in the next ten days, and other Commonwealth troops.

THE PILGRIM TRUST

The Pilgrim Trust's first project was the shoring up of Durham Cathedral.

MEN WITHOUT WORK

A Report made to the Pilgrim Trust

WITH AN
Introduction by the
ARCHBISHOP OF YORK
and a Preface by
LORD MACMILLAN

CAMBRIDGE
AT THE UNIVERSITY PRESS
1938

The Pilgrim Trust has made a £5,000 grant to the Zoological Society of London to enable informative labels to be attached to the cages and dens of aviaries, menageries and paddocks, and more for answering common questions received by intelligent and curious visitors. Enamel labels have been proposed for the exhibits in both Regent's Park and Whipsnade.

The Pilgrim Trust was set up in 1930 by Edward Harkness, an American philanthropist, whose family traced its roots to Dumfriesshire. He retained a lifelong love of Great Britain and after British contribution to the First World War, donated £2 million to create the Trust wanting it to support the urgent future needs of the country. This gift captured the country's imagination, and the King and Queen received him and his wife at Buckingham Palace. In 1931, the Trust's first grant of £25,000 went to Durham Castle, which with shifting foundations, was in urgent need of work to save the building from sliding into the River Wear. Much of their early work focused on the high levels of unemployment in the country and giving individuals work and volunteering opportunities. The report they commissioned, 'Men Without Work', which explored the unemployed across six towns, was a significant piece of research, designed to provide the Pilgrim Trustees with guidance on the allocation of funding in relation to the social problems associated with unemployment.

At the outbreak of the War, an ambitious scheme was set up to employ artists on the home front. This was the brainchild of Sir Kenneth Clark working together with the Pilgrim Trust. The result is a collection of more than 1,500 watercolours and drawings that make up a record of British lives and landscapes at a time of imminent change. Now, they actively pursue the preservation and restoration of the nation's heritage of beautiful things.

OCT 15TH - 21ST 1945

IN THE NEWS

Monday 15   **"Army to Police"** The Minister of War has announced that five thousand servicemen are eligible to leave the armed forces to become policemen. The offer comes following a report showing a 16,000-person shortage in the police force.

Tuesday 16   **"The Penicillin Train"** The Penicillin Exhibition, located in a GWR train, is to be at Paddington Station over the next week where it will continue its money raising drive. More than £2,000 has been collected whilst the train has been on tour.

Wednesday 17   **"Big US Food Supplies"** Large quantities of food being shipped from the United States is to be added to the British allocation. The shipment includes over 240 million tons of meat, 360 million lbs of flour and 30 million lbs of tinned fish.

Thursday 18   **"Wine Imports"** The Ministry of Food is to begin the importation of wines from the Dominions and the Continent. Negotiations are nearing a close for the purchase of South African, French, and Algerian wine.

Friday 19   **"Make Room"** People across Britain with spare bedrooms have been asked by the Government to be prepared to accept men who have been demobbed, if extra accommodation is needed.

Saturday 20   **"Satellite Towns"** The Government has announced plans to commence the building of *Satellite Towns,* with work beginning on the Stevenage site in under two years. The Ministry of Town and Country Planning is to set up a government-supported corporation for the development.

Sunday 21   **"One Million Radios"** Britain is set to produce in excess of one million radios in the next twelve months. Although not at the pre-war levels of 1.4 million, over half of these are earmarked to be exported to the Continent.

HERE IN BRITAIN

"The British Stars and Stripes"

The British edition of the American *Stars and Stripes* newspaper is to publish its last edition this week. The publication, started with the arrival of American troops in London, has been popular amongst US troops and the British public alike. Intent on keeping the world up to date with war developments.

American journalists used the printing offices of the Times Newspaper. The troops felt so at home in the offices that one of them was heard to say, *"The Times? Oh yes, it's produced in our building.'*

AROUND THE WORLD

"The Lady with the Shawl"

With Stockholm boasting one of the most famous opera houses in the world, it is little wonder that the people of Sweden are staunch lovers of the events. There is one woman however, who appears to love it more than most.

At the age of 75, Mrs Runnback has clocked up over 7,000 visits to the opera, and is still going strong. She is well known across the city for waving her shawl furiously from her gallery seat at the end of each performance earning her the nickname, *The Lady with the Shawl.*

TRAFALGAR DAY

Sunday 21st October
Trafalgar Day Lunch

Join us to commemorate
Nelson's famous victory

"Admiral Nelson Would Have Been Proud" was the message delivered by the First Lord of the Admiralty, speaking at the annual Trafalgar Day lunch of the Navy League. His speech highlighted the work of the navy during the war, using it to justify how sea power has never been more important than now. Trafalgar Day is an annual celebration observed on October 21, commemorating the Royal Navy's victory over the French and Spanish at the Battle of Trafalgar in 1805. Even though France was the dominant military force, led by Napoleon, the Royal Navy ruled the seas, and, in this battle, Nelson captured 18 French ships, forcing a French surrender.

Nevertheless, the Battle of Trafalgar is perhaps remembered most for the death of Admiral Horatio Nelson aboard HMS Victory. His body was placed in a cask of brandy mixed with camphor and myrrh, which was then lashed to the Victory's mainmast and placed under guard. At Gibraltar the body was transferred to a lead-lined coffin filled with spirits of wine. Arriving eventually at the Nore on the Thames, Nelson's body was placed inside a lead coffin which was encased in a wood made from the mast of his ship 'L'Orient', salvaged after his greatest victory, the Battle of the Nile. After a four-hour service at St. Paul's Cathedral, he was finally interred within the crypt, in a black marble sarcophagus originally carved for Cardinal Wolsey.

Nelson's skill and bravery was such that he was claimed a national hero, with many monuments erected throughout Britain in the years following his death. On Trafalgar Day, his monuments are decorated with flags, banners or laurel swags, and wreath laying ceremonies are held in his honour when the famous Trafalgar flag signal "England expects that every man will do his duty" is flown from Nelson's Column in London.

IN THE NEWS

Monday 22 — **"Across England in 29 Minutes"** The first of two jets that will try for the world's air speed record attempt, flew from Gloucester to Kent in a total flying time of just 29 minutes. The two-leg journey saw the Meteor pass over London Bridge at 2,000 feet.

Tuesday 23 — **"People's Budget"** The Government has introduced the first 'People's Budget' intent on spurring production to increase export trade. The Chancellor, speaking about raising the national income, wanted to *'give the workers an incentive to raise their earnings.'*

Wednesday 24 — **"Bypasses"** The Ministry of War Transport has announced plans for over 1,000 miles of 'fast roads' which would bypass cities and towns and reduce the ever-increasing road death toll. During the war, there was an alarming, average number of 20 deaths per day, four of which were children.

Thursday 25 — **"Towns Afloat"** Hundreds of people have been left homeless across Southern England as gales and floods hit towns. Some areas have been left 5 ft deep in sea water. Thankfully, the worst hit areas were evacuated before the devastation.

Friday 26 — **"Nobel Prize"** The Nobel Prize for Medicine this year has been awarded jointly to Sir Alexander Fleming, and Sir Howard Florey for their discovery of penicillin.

Saturday 27 — **"The Dock Strike Endures"** The number of dock workers on strike has reached over 46,000 as the dispute enters its third week of chaos. Approximately two thirds of the nation's dock labour force is idle.

Sunday 28 — **"Whaling Steamer"** The first British Whaling Steamer since before the war has left the Tees heading directly to South Georgia. The Southern Venturer, some 14,000 tons, will transport whale oil and experimental whale meat.

HERE IN BRITAIN

"Pyrethrum Decontrolled"

The control of pyrethrum, a toxic insecticide, is to be decontrolled following an announcement by the Ministry of Supply. Civilians may now obtain the war office acquired pyrethrum flowers without a license. The Ministry's current stock of flowers may be obtained from the Director of Sundry Materials, Ministry of Supply. During the war, pyrethrum was used as a preservative for stored foods and as protection against malaria for troops in tropical countries. The seed is native to Kenya and was one of their principal war exports.

AROUND THE WORLD

"Bee Smugglers"

Rice, raw silk and other valuable products are making their way across the Swiss border in large quantities, but it is the transportation of honey by one trader that has piqued the interest of many. After the prohibition of the export of Italian honey, a Swiss man lobbied his Italian vendor to bring honey pots to just the other side of the barbed wire border; he moved his own beehives 1,000 yards from the honey and within three days, the Swiss man's bees had smuggled some 200lbs worth of honey across the border.

The Flying Tadpole

The Miles Aerovan (main). George Miles, its designer (inset).

One of the most unusual, yet versatile, aircraft ever produced by British manufacturing, the Miles Aerovan, is to be used to aid export trade in plans released by the Ministry of Transport. This week, an Aerovan landed in Zurich containing over 5,000 fountain pens and is scheduled to give demonstration flights across Switzerland and France later this month. The aircraft, nicknamed the *Flying Tadpole,* has a quirky appearance, but, while its looks may deceive, the Aerovan is extremely versatile, capable of transporting up to ten passengers, goods, and could be used as an air ambulance or even a flying caravan.

The design was conceived by George Miles towards the end of the war, to meet the expected and ongoing increase in demand for air travel and without prior permission from the Air Ministry, he drew up plans and prototypes for the Miles Aerovan. The design was intended by Miles to serve as troop and supply carriers in the Far East during the war, and to then double as civilian airliners after, but the unconventional design was put on hold by the Ministry until now because of its unsanctioned 'birth'. The unusual aeroplane is made predominantly from wood with a high wing and tail design and large rear clam shell doors, helping to gain its name *The Flying Tadpole,* but it wasn't until January this year that a full working prototype made its debut. The original square windows have since been replaced by round porthole ones, and the Berkshire factory has been working round the clock to produce the quota authorised by the Government.

IN THE NEWS

Monday 29   **"The First Farnborough Air Show"** The Royal Aircraft Establishment in Farnborough, today put on the biggest display of military and civilian aircraft ever seen in England.

Tuesday 30   **"World Youth Conference"** Messages from both the King and President Truman were read aloud to those in attendance at the inauguration of the World Youth Conference. Representatives from over 60 countries will visit the Royal Albert Hall over the next week.

Wednesday 31   **"Lincoln's Inn"** Queen Mary attended celebrations marking the centenary of the opening of the Great Hall, Lincoln's Inn which Queen Victoria opened 100 years ago. Queen Mary signed the 'Golden Book', using the same inkstand provided for Queen Victoria at the opening.

Thursday 1   **"Swing to the Left"** Labour gains in the recent municipal elections show the British public fully commit to a 'swing to the left' after early results saw Conservative and Liberal defeats across the country. Whilst Labour was very successful, only seven out of 144 Communist Party candidates were elected.

Friday 2   **"Food to Germany"** The British controlled zone in Germany is to be sent a limited supply of unused, surplus army rations, for the civil population.

Saturday 3   **"Oranges for Christmas"** Over 800,000 cases of citrus fruit, mainly oranges, will be shipped from Palestine to Britain by Christmas. It marks the first Palestinian crop to be shipped for over six years.

Sunday 4   **"Air Speed Attempt"** Changeable conditions repeatedly hindered the world air speed record attempt at Manston Aerodrome, disappointing those who had come to watch. Morning trial flights indicated speeds of well over 400 mph were achievable.

HERE IN BRITAIN

"Fabric Fortissimos"

During the war Britain led the way in fabric research, and it appears that the post war industry is no different. Fabrics are lighter and brighter and the tweed suits of the future can be reduced in weight by over a quarter, whilst still retaining their trademark warmth.

New Scottish wool designs are among the projects on display at the International Wool Secretariat in London, the leading attraction being Dream Touch, a gay fabric, golden, of very light texture with a small percentage of angora to give it velvety smoothness.

AROUND THE WORLD

"Jill the Platypus"

In Melbourne, Australia, 'Jill,' known fondly as the world's favourite platypus, has set another new record by building a nest and laying two eggs, stuck together in platypus manner to prevent them rolling about.

Jill made history two years ago by becoming the first platypus to hatch an egg in public. This time the eggs have been taken from her because they are wanted for scientific purposes, to find out whether a platypus will lay twice in one season, and also because the sanctuary cannot afford to keep more of the species.

SHIPWRIGHTS COMPANY

The Guilds and Livery Companies of the City of London originated in the 11th century by craftsmen in mutual support in their respective trades, this practice was followed by the merchants

WITHIN THE ARK SAFE FOR EVER

THE GUILDS AND LIVERY COMPANIES OF THE CITY OF LONDON

A court of the Shipwrights' Company luncheon was held at the Mansion House this month, where the King, as 'Permanent Master' gave a speech to all those in attendance. He then presided over the meeting of the court when the honorary freedom of the Company was conferred on Winston Churchill. The former Prime Minister spoke of the great honour he felt at being made a member of the ancient company, '*whose roots date back to the early Plantagenets and whose activities to-day were abreast of the most modern developments*'.

The title of 'Livery Company' dates back as early as the first Guilds in the 12th Century with the earliest charter still in existence being granted to the Weavers' Company in 1155. As society developed, and the earliest forms of British capitalism grew, these Guilds became more individualised, often characterising themselves by specific clothes, or liveries, to distinguish themselves from other Guilds. By the 14th Century, there were 48 well-established companies that had earned political influence with the Lord Mayor through charters and ordinances. They enjoyed their status, the bill of fare of a Livery Company feast of 1506 was quoted by the Master of the Company and included '36 chickens, one swan, four geese, nine rabbits, two rumps of beef, four breasts of veal, 50 eggs, and 30 gallons of Gascoyne wine.'

Now, livery companies are one of the cornerstones for political operation in London, responsible for the election of Sheriffs of the City of London and they hold large influence with the mayor. The Worshipful Company of Shipwrights' was originally formed to safeguard the quality of shipbuilding in London, the earliest surviving written reference occurs in the records of the City of London in the reign of King Richard II in 1387.

IN THE NEWS

Monday 5 **"End of the Strike"** After three long weeks, the dockworkers strike has finally come to an end, and ports across Britain swung back into action. During the strike, 43,000 men lay idle, and 21,000 soldiers were drafted in to supplement the loss of manpower.

Tuesday 6 **"Standing in"** Bus crews in London have taken the regulations surrounding the carrying of standing passengers into their own hands, by preventing anyone standing between the hours of 9:30 and 4:30.

Wednesday 7 **"World Air Speed Record"** After weather prohibited the attempt last week, Herne Bay was at last the site of the official breaking of the world air speed record. Two Meteor Jets averaged a speed of over 600mph.

Thursday 8 " **X-Ray Anniversary"** The fiftieth anniversary of Roentgen's discovery of X-Rays was celebrated today by the Royal Society, who held an all-day conference in London. The event was attended by British, Swedish, French and Dutch scientists.

Friday 9 **"Lord Mayor's Show"** A mile long procession escorted the new Mayor of London from Guildhall to the Law Courts where he took the oath presented to him by judges. The ancient tradition has been restored in a new post-war format.

Saturday 10 **"Jobless Clergy"** The Church of England is in the unusual position of not being able to find jobs for its clergy men. Returning from war service, Chaplains and other higher-ranking officials have been left without places to be based.

Sunday 11 **"The King at the Cenotaph"** London's first official act of commemoration for those who died during *both* wars was held today at the Cenotaph in London and marked by all across Britain on Remembrance Day.

HERE IN BRITAIN

"Forgotten Supplies"

Complaints have come in from across the country of 'forgotten' emergency supplies, placed in countless secure locations at the start of the war, and now deteriorating at a time when the need for these rest centres and civil casualty stations has passed and when there is an urgent demand for such things as blankets, mattresses and beds.

Berkshire is a major culprit, as although the requisitioned buildings closed down last Spring, they are still yet to be cleared. Local authorities are powerless to intervene, as they await instructions from the Ministry of Health.

AROUND THE WORLD

"Japanese Treasures for Food"

Emperor Hirohito has informed the Japanese Government that he is prepared to sell his personal art collection to help finance the importation of much needed food for the starving population. The collection features artwork dating back hundreds of years. The Empress has also offered her extensive collection of jewels, and the Government has urged wealthy Japanese business owners to follow the unprecedented example of their rulers to help raise the necessary funds. The government immediately drafted a letter to General MacArthur conveying the offer.

Across the world, the first peacetime Remembrance Sunday commemorating those who died in both World Wars was marked in many different.

Berlin: A two-minute silence in Berlin was observed for the first time as the city, under allied occupation, fell quiet at 1pm, which was 11am in London. Berlin's now-familiar air raid sirens marked the beginning of the period, which saw the city remain in complete silence throughout with the exception of one policeman, who broke the quiet by telling a passer-by to stop and remove his hat.

Paris: 15 symbolic coffins of known and named people, who died fighting for the French Resistance movement were brought to, and placed around, Napoleon's tomb at Les Invalides before being transported to the Arc de Triomphe on gun carriages. General De Gaulle gave an emotional speech talking of France's commitment to her own protection and spoke of the need to unite to collectively heal the country's wounds from the last 30 years of war.

Tokyo: The first Armistice Day ceremonies in the city since 1941 were held in the grounds of the British Embassy. The ceremony was observed by a small number of British and Australian army and navy officers, and a select number of war correspondents situated in the country. A small number of Japanese staff, along with 15 Swiss Diplomats were also in attendance.

Similar services took place in Canada, Australia, Egypt, Malta and even Jerusalem, as the reach of both 20th Century conflicts proved their 'World War' titles by touching all corners of the globe.

IN THE NEWS

Monday 12   **"Parachute Clothing"** 26 million yards of nylon, cotton and Celanese fabrics have been surrendered as surplus by the armed forces, who held the material for the creation of parachutes. Instead, the fabrics will be re-purposed and used for much needed clothes production.

Tuesday 13   **"Extra Christmas Rations"** The Minister of Food has announced that the ration allowance per person will increase over Christmas by one pound of sugar, four ounces of chocolate and sweets, six ounces of margarine and butter, and by an extra six-penny worth of meat.

Wednesday 14   **"Roll of Honour"** St Paul's Cathedral is to be the host of a proposed permanent memorial to American soldiers who lost their lives whilst being based in the British Isles.

Thursday 15   **"Cigarettes for Overseas"** The NAAFI has announced that cigarette provisions for British forces still overseas is to increase to 75 per man, per week.

Friday 16   **"Royal Victory Tour"** The King and Queen were welcomed by a guard of honour when they arrived in Cardiff at the beginning of their tour of South Wales. The Welsh Regiment was joined by their mascot goat, who remained kneeling, with head bowed, during the national anthem.

Saturday 17   **"Underground Factory"** Details have been revealed by the Royal Institute of British Architects of a factory built completely underground in Britain during the war. Both the cost and time of building was the same as for a surface factory.

Sunday 18   **"Teacher Training"** The Ministry of Education has expressed the need to speed up the teacher recruitment and training process with a bill being passed unanimously at the annual conference of the Workers' Educational Association. There is a need for as many as 70,000 more teachers.

HERE IN BRITAIN

"Long Socks Again"

The government provision restricting the length of men's socks is to be lifted, following an announcement by the Ministry of Trade. The restriction was originally imposed in 1942, due to the dire need for yarn to help with the creation of uniforms, warm clothes and equipment for the services, and in the four years since, it is thought that over 6 million lbs of the material has been saved. Though the restrictions have been lifted, manufacturers have warned that it will be many months before long socks will be seen again in shops.

AROUND THE WORLD

"PM's Private Plane"

Former Prime Minister Mr Churchill has been forced to return the plane gifted to him by the late President Roosevelt last year due to its high running costs. Returning the aircraft to the United States *'with regrets'*, Mr Churchill emphasised how public funds are not available given he is no longer Prime Minister, and it was too expensive to justify alone. The plane, equipped with a conference table, kitchen, and cocktail cabinet, needed over £25,000 of repairs and now sits idle in Washington whilst the State Department ponder what to do with it.

WOMEN'S LAND ARMY

The story of British farming during the war years is to be collated and told through an ornate booklet entitled *'The Land at War.'* Prepared by the Ministry of Information, the pamphlet will act as a deserving tribute to the work of the woman-led farming workforce during the war, which turned the British agricultural industry into one of the most highly mechanised in the world. Over six million additional acres of cultivated land were utilised and the Sussex Downs yielded their first crops since the Saxon days.

The Land Army girls were a mobile force of women ready to undertake all kinds of farm work in any part of the country. They wore their distinctive uniform and were normally employed and paid by the individual farmers, but the organisation supervised their lodging arrangement and their general welfare. Replacing male farm workers who had gone to war, the women came from all walks of life and despite having little or no agricultural experience, they were found ploughing fields, growing the produce, milking the cows, catching the rats, driving the tractors and much, much more. There was also an 'army' of women who, unable because of domestic commitments to travel or live away, offered their services for work in their home district, and all on minimum wage. In 1941, *'In the Event of Invasion'*, Land Girls were encouraged to stick to their jobs, but advice was also issued on how to disable tractors if in real danger of capture by the enemy.

This quotation from Lady Denman, the Director of the Women's Land Army, summarises the importance of the Land Girls. *'The land army fights in the fields. It is in the fields of Britain that the most critical battle of the present war may well be fought and won.'*

Nov 19TH - 25TH 1945

IN THE NEWS

Monday 19 **"Triumph for British Motorcycles"** The first British export of £100,000 worth of Triumph motorbikes to the United States since the war is ready to ship. American agents are ready to place much bigger orders once the first shipment is delivered.

Tuesday 20 **"PM Diverted"** The Prime Minister, Mr Attlee, was diverted from his scheduled airport when returning from his visit to Canada as thick fog covered Southern England. Landing at Tangmere instead of Northolt, the Prime Minister ended up being just four minutes behind schedule.

Wednesday 21 **"Whaling Conference"** An international whaling conference is being held in London to discuss any necessary modifications to the 1937 Whaling Agreement ahead of the 1946-47 season. The conference has representatives from across the world.

Thursday 22 **"Thanksgiving"** The first American Thanksgiving Day since total victory was celebrated in England as well as America, as 3,000 US servicemen attended a special service at Westminster Abbey.

Friday 23 **"Multi-Carrier Amplitude Modulation"** A new system of mobile radio to be used across short ranges has been perfected by the Home Office. The design is to be implemented in police forces patrolling large country areas.

Saturday 24 **"Telephone Demand"** The Chairman of the Telecommunication Engineering and Manufacturing Association, speaking at their annual dinner, spoke of the 250,000-person waiting list wanting to get their hands on a telephone for their own home.

Sunday 25 **"Steel Mill for Teesside"** Teesside, one of the development areas marked in the Distribution of Industry Bill, is to be the site of a pioneering new English steel mill, the first in the country to use the most-up-to-date method of structural steel construction.

HERE IN BRITAIN
"Trolley Birth"

Queen Charlotte's Maternity Hospital at Stamford Brook, London, has been forced to 'turn away expectant mothers at the rate of 4,000 a year' in alarming figures published by the institution. Just last week, 17 mothers were forced to give birth on trolleys and mattresses because all the beds in the hospital were full. Given the modern nature of the hospital, designed to set an example to all across the world of an efficient Maternity ward layout, the £500,000 project's failure to accommodate the influx of mothers does not have the desired international effect.

AROUND THE WORLD
"Tsetse Fly"

Ongoing experiments as to the best way to eradicate the tsetse fly, currently infesting large portions of the African continent, have concluded that DDT is the most effective chemical for extermination. The Department of Agriculture in South Africa has reported that the chemical does not rule out the possibility of complete eradication, as it appears to only affect specific species of flies, not crickets, grasshoppers, or mantis. Although the test spray, carried out over 25 square miles, showed that more of the chemical was required, the preliminary tests were positive.

FIDO

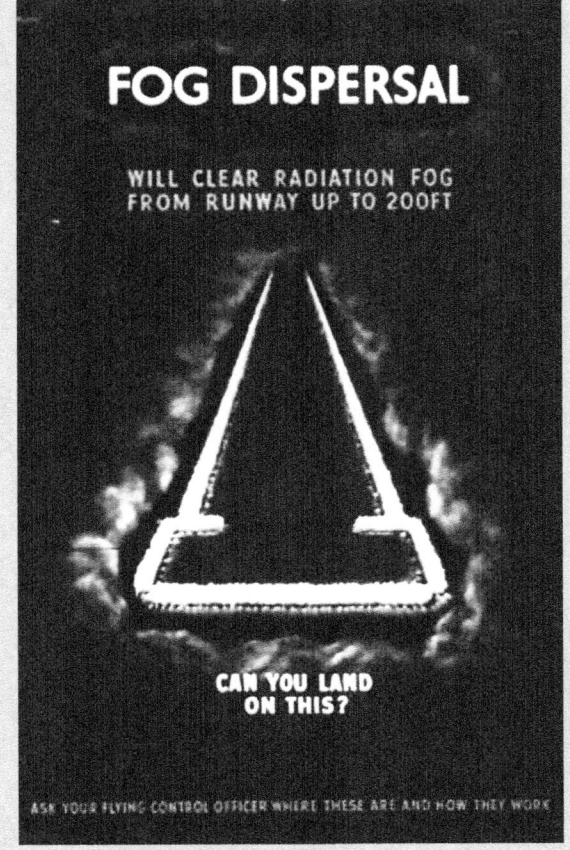

FOG DISPERSAL

WILL CLEAR RADIATION FOG
FROM RUNWAY UP TO 200FT

CAN YOU LAND
ON THIS?

ASK YOUR FLYING CONTROL OFFICER WHERE THESE ARE AND HOW THEY WORK

FLYING THROUGH FIRE

FIDO – THE FOGBUSTER OF WORLD WAR TWO

GEOFFREY WILLIAMS

*Freeing the RAF's Airfields
from the Fog Menace*

FOREWORD BY MARSHAL OF THE RAF
SIR MICHAEL BEETHAM GCB CBE DFC AFC FRAeS

The Minister in charge of Petroleum Warfare who, under former Prime Minister Mr Churchill, was responsible for a number of fog dispersal developments during the war, announced this week the decision of the Ministry of Civil Aviation to stop work on the FIDO fog dispenser, on the grounds of economic viability. Already half completed at Heathrow airport, the Fog Investigation and Dispersal Operation, would have to run for long periods of time, at a high cost, to be at all effective - a cost which the government feels better placed in other areas of public spending.

The device was originally designed to help alleviate fog for RAF Bomber Command aircraft returning from air raids, and the investigation as to its possible commercial uses has been continued by the government. Heat was determined the key to fog clearance, therefore FIDO equipped airfields had runways lined with fuel tanks, pipes and a series of burners that could be turned on and off on demand. When lit, the burners used over one hundred thousand gallons of fuel every hour, roaring and shooting flames so high into the air that they could be seen for over 60 miles. The system was capable of dispersing even the thickest fog within minutes.

Fog, besides the Luftwaffe, was one of the RAF's most formidable enemies during the war, often causing delays, disruption and in some cases, death and destruction, making the job assigned to the Petroleum Warfare Department of the utmost importance. General advice to bomber aircraft crews caught out by thick fog was to fly back to sea but bail out whilst still over land, meaning the aircraft crashed into the ocean. Naturally this was neither a cost efficient nor safe alternative to landing, and with sorties often involving several hundred aircraft, it was not a sustainable procedure.

IN THE NEWS

Monday 26 — **"Go-Slow Gas Workers"** Over 1,000 men employed by the Gas and Light Coke Company have gone on strike following an announcement by the corporation that it would dismiss anyone who continues to 'go slow' on night shifts.

Tuesday 27 — **"Corsets by Christmas"** The war-to-peacetime industry switch has occurred far quicker than first anticipated, with nylon underwear set to be back in shops by the end of the week. Glamorous nightdresses line London's shop windows once again, and corsets are to be available before Christmas.

Wednesday 28 — **"Self-Confessed Traitor"** John Amery was sentenced to death just eight minutes after entering the Central Criminal Court, having been found guilty of high treason earlier this month.

Thursday 29 — **"Flying Boat"** The first British flying-boat to be built since the war was launched at Rochester. Capable of speeds in excess of 190mph and a range of 2,200 miles, the new design, named the Sandringham, can seat 24 passengers in luxurious conditions.

Friday 30 — **"Dry November"** The driest November for over 100 years has ended with just seven millilitres of rainfall at Kew Observatory over the last 30 days. The last time there was this little rain was during November 1858.

Saturday 1 — **"Christmas Demobilisation Interval"** Over the Christmas break, releases from the Army and Navy will be almost entirely suspended due to the lack of transport. No one will be collected from Army Home Commands on Christmas Eve, Christmas Day or Boxing Day.

Sunday 2 — **"Air Crash Inquiry"** An official Inquiry has been opened after the prototype Handley Page Hermes four engine airliner crashed on an initial test flight near Radlett railway station.

HERE IN BRITAIN

"Atomic Car"

The Minister of Fuel and Power went to Westminster this week to test the first, fully working, atomic car, only to find the vehicle in an undriveable condition. The inventor, Dr Wilson, stated that the car, which had been left outside his office on Regent Street, had been 'sabotaged' by a rival inventor, who broke two vital components. Suspicions point to individuals apprehensive about the effect an atomic car might have on industry, but nonetheless Dr Wilson has assured MPs that he will have a working vehicle within the month.

AROUND THE WORLD

"Forbidden Sports"

The Allied Command in Berlin has prohibited the organisation or sponsoring of specific sports including boxing, mountain climbing, trapeze work, rowing, weightlifting and athletics lest they might be vessels for Nazi military drills. Instead, the allies have offered the Germans replacements like rugby, football, tennis, fishing, and callisthenics, as these are not seen to *promote military preparedness*'. The rule comes from Russian command, who were undoubtedly mindful of the secret drilling done by the Nazis through sport before the war.

THE BOYS' CLUBS

*A south coast club outing.
The landing craft has been loaded and the
boys, and a few girls, are ready for the off.
A Royal Marine supervises.*

The Prime Minister Clement Attlee attended a dinner organised by the National Association of Boys' Clubs, where he outlined the story of one of the most human and unselfish episodes of the war. At the meeting of some 2,500 captured allied soldiers in Oflag 17 prisoner of war camp in Brunswick, the men, who were starving, cold, wet and unsure about when they would be liberated, agreed that, when the war ended, a club should be set up to help poor and underprivileged boys in Britain. The Prime Minister spoke of one man in particular, a private captured at Arnhem, whose enthusiasm for the project ultimately convinced those in the room still sceptical about the idea. £13,000 was raised there and then, with a pledge of a further £700 a year towards the programme, and as much as £5 coming out of each man's pay voluntarily, most of whom were Privates.

Lord Aberdare, Chairman of the Association, said, '*now a great revolution was taking place and we could never go back. The country has, perhaps, passed through the greatest period in our history and has entered a new age where it was accepted that society would to a larger extent than before, be planned. But if freedom is denied in one sphere, it should be secured elsewhere. If our industrial and economic life and education is to be largely planned, then leisure life must be the place for the exercise of real freedom. 'To put it in practical terms, the club must show the boy the joy of that coordination of hand and eye which made a perfect stroke at cricket, the sheer physical satisfaction which came from a hard-fought game, the creative satisfactions of arts and crafts, and the intellectual satisfactions of drama and literature.*'

DEC 3RD - DEC 9TH 1945

IN THE NEWS

Monday 3   **"Hotel Release"** Over 1,500 of the total 1,759 hotels and guest houses held by the War Department for use during the conflict are to be derequisitioned by next February leaving just 250 still under government ownership.

Tuesday 4   **"Christmas Meat Strike"** Workers at Smithfield Meat Market are threatening to put down their cleavers over Christmas unless the London Wholesale Meat Supply Association agree to reinstate all returning servicemen to their former roles.

Wednesday 5   **"Aircraft Can-Carrier"** The first jet propelled aircraft has successfully landed on the flight deck of HMS Ocean just off the Isle of Wight. The new Naval aircraft, the Vampire, made an efficient landing on board the moving 14,000-ton vessel.

Thursday 6   **"Expensive Rebuild"** An agreement between the House of Commons and the White House was announced by the Prime Minister, assuring Great Britain over $4 billion (c.£1 billion) from the US to help rebuild the country.

Friday 7   **"The Red Cross"** It has been reported that during the war, the Red Cross and St John War Organisation, sent a colossal 19,326,000 food parcels to prisoners of war on the continent; the charity became the single largest distributor of goods besides the Army Ordnance.

Saturday 8   **"The Home of Razor Slashing"** The BBC has been forced to apologise for referring to Gorbals as the *'dockland of Glasgow, home of the razor slashing gangs'.* The *'irresponsible and unwarranted slur'* drew protest from many Scottish political figures.

Sunday 9   **"Guinea Pigs"** Civil Servants from the Ministry of Food, evacuated to Colwyn Bay from London in 1940, and called 'guinea pigs' because householders with whom they were billeted received 21s. a week, returned to London yesterday.

HERE IN BRITAIN

"Excessive Spit and Polish"

A Labour MP has raised the issue of alleged unnecessary drills, fatigues and parades. Mr Mikardo said that *'many officers in the Army did not yet realise that our soldiers were now a cross-section of the whole nation, who did not leave their thinking caps off when they put their Army caps on'.* He did not ask for relaxation of duties necessary for order and discipline but sought that the workers in uniform should be treated like those not in uniform, as thinking and sensible human beings.

AROUND THE WORLD

"The Great Wave"

Over 4,000 people are thought to have been killed and a further 40,000 rendered homeless after a great wave washed away over 100 miles of Indian coastline. Harrowing images of corpses being washed up on beaches, and villages left in ruins, are growing in number daily as rescue missions continue to find survivors. The wave struck in the night, and many were killed in their sleep. Onlookers spoke of *'thousands of pebbles being thrown into the air like bullets'* as bodies were tossed about by the water.

PENNIES FOR CHRISTMAS

At Christmastime, even during a war, more money is spent than at any other time of the year. Christmas spending even exceeds that of August Bank Holiday, which ranks as the second spending season. During this week the public expenditure on presents, extra provisions, railway fares, and amusements, touches its peak. All the notes and coin in the country are called into circulation. That is why new money is usually more abundant at Christmas than at any other time, which is a good thing, as new coins are especially popular as Christmas-boxes. At one time banks went to considerable trouble to ensure that all their branches received a quantity of new money at Christmas but in recent years this has been impossible as minting has been suspended during the war to save copper for munitions. This Christmas, however, is the first since 1939 that new pennies have been in circulation.

The Christmas penny received its first blow in 1922. During the 1914-18 war such vast quantities of pennies were struck that, with the post-war fall in prices, millions became surplus and unwanted. The minting of pennies was suspended and there were no new ones for the Christmases of 1922, 1923, and 1924. In 1934 public demand revived and pennies were struck again but the Royal Mint found itself in a dilemma. Some banks had plenty of old pennies whilst other banks were short and were to be supplied with new ones. To prevent any heartbreak, the Mint darkened all its 1934 pennies with photographic hypo (sodium thiosulfate) so that they looked like old ones. This was so successful that their subterfuge has been repeated this year as the authorities feared, not without cause, that bright pennies would be hoarded until Christmas instead of doing their duty as coins of the realm.

DEC 10TH - DEC 16TH 1945

IN THE NEWS

Monday 10   **"Waterloo Bridge"** The new Waterloo Bridge was officially opened despite the bridge being open for pedestrians for over three years, and traffic since November last year, an official ceremony was now deemed appropriate.

Tuesday 11   **"More Bobbies on the Beat"** Scotland Yard has increased the number of constables on beat duties, and more traffic police to catch unauthorised drivers entering and leaving London by car.

Wednesday 12 **"Black Cabs"** A new design for London taxis has been released, with planned modifications in several areas. The taxicabs of the future will have a lower roof, wider seating allocation and an improved, illuminated, *For Hire* sign.

Thursday 13   **"The Crime Wave"** Both Scotland Yard and the Metropolitan Police are confident that the recent increase in serious crime can be reduced with the help of the general public. Although the figures remain lower than they were following the end of World War I.

Friday 14   **"Identity Check"** Servicemen and visitors to restaurants and theatres had their identity checked by police who were looking for deserters from both British and American forces.

Saturday 15   **"Docked Pay"** A minimum days wage of 19s. has been agreed by the leaders of the mining unions and employers so that further negotiations might be opened. A permanent scheme of decasualisation is to be discussed in the new year.

Sunday 16   **"National Theatre"** There are plans for the erection of a Shakespeare Memorial National Theatre on the Southbank of the Thames, midway between Hungerford Bridge and Waterloo Bridge.

HERE IN BRITAIN

"Comfort for Seamen"

Over 300,000 knitters met in London where they were thanked for their contributions to the Merchant Navy Comforts Service over the last six years. Since 1940, over 8 million gifts were sent overseas to men of the British and Allied Merchant Navies, including nearly 4 million knitted garments.

The representatives were presented with badges commemorating a special service to the war effort in London. Of the knitters present, two were men, both aged over 70, one of whom had knitted 115 pullovers.

AROUND THE WORLD

"Australian Lights out at 9pm"

Coal strikes across New South Wales have forced authorities to impose restrictions on energy usage for the foreseeable future. Lights out in all dwellings must be no later than 9pm; the wireless will be restricted to just one hour per day; cooking may only take place between 5:30 and 7pm; church services will be required to run under candlelight, and newspaper printing has been suspended. These restrictions were vital to ensure a sufficient electricity and gas supply, which would have run out by the end of this week if not imposed.

THE REGENCY SOCIETY

The Royal Pavilion Brighton

A society has been formed in Brighton and Hove to stem indiscriminate destruction of Regency buildings. Amidst proposed plans for the development of many southern towns and cities across Britain, there are a select few which have highlighted the importance of preserving Britain's rich Regency history. Brighton has become the first place targeted by the Society, who say it is of vital importance to retain the *narrow little streets* of the old town and *harness the past to the future*. The aim of the society is to avoid the sites becoming museum pieces of the future, instead, remaining a quintessential part of Britain that, in 20 years' time, travellers from across the world might visit.

A land mark of Brighton since the 18th Century, the Marine Pavilion was first commissioned by George IV in 1786, when the then young King expressed a desire for a residence in the town. It was actually the King's cook who first purchased the seaside house, along with a substantial area of seafront land. Given Brighton's growing prestige as an aristocratic resort, and the King's fondness for the town after visiting to cure his gout some five years prior, the Pavilion became a serene respite for the Royal Family for more almost a century.

After being converted to a residence more fit for royalty by the architect Henry Holland, the neo-classical Pavilion became home to royal entertainment for three generations of monarchy. King George IV, William IV and finally Queen Victoria all resided in the Pavilion, though it was the Queen who sold the building to the Corporation of Brighton in 1846, instead preferring Osbourne House on the Isle of Wight. Nevertheless, the Pavilion remained useful, with the proceeds from its sale going towards furnishing both Buckingham Palace and Windsor Castle.

DEC 17TH - DEC 23RD 1945

IN THE NEWS

Monday 17   **"Moscow Conference"** The first meeting between the foreign ministers of Great Britain, The US and Russia took place in Moscow. Due to the complexity of the negotiations and the variety of the topics to be debated, the talks are expected to be prolonged.

Tuesday 18   **"Mistletoe for Christmas"** The first consignment of mistletoe to be shipped to Britain for six years arrived at Tower Bridge in time for Christmas, along with a large cargo of oranges for distribution across London.

Wednesday 19 **"War Decorations"** Since the beginning of the war, the King has personally presented more than 44,000 decorations to deserving people. With a further 55,000 needing to be bestowed, the medals will now be posted with a signed letter.

Thursday 20   **"'The Few'"** The White Hart Inn in Brasted has opened a memorial to 'the few' who defended the country during the Battle of Britain. The unofficial HQ for Fighter Command during 1940, the back of the bar parlour is covered with scrawled signatures from visiting airmen.

Friday 21   **"Christmas Gifts"** The Minister of Food has distributed some of the 105,000 Christmas puddings donated by South Africa, to 2,000 poor people in Bermondsey, with more scheduled to be sent to the needy in other parts of Britain.

Saturday 22   **"The Christmas Rush"** All the big London stations were exceptionally busy yesterday with the start of Christmas holiday traffic, but much larger numbers of passengers, going away or travelling home for their first peace-time Christmas for six years, are expected today.

Sunday 23   **"Minor Inconvenience"** Several mines have been washed up on the shores of Southern England due to the rough seas and persistent winds.

HERE IN BRITAIN

"Heartbreak Corner"

At Mount Pleasant sorting office in London, there is an area where the Christmas mail casualties are dealt with. Commonly, the turkey left with only a string round its neck to indicate that it once bore a label and paper covering, or the food parcel packaging burst by loose tins. Where they can, staff attach fresh string, paper, gum and labels to help them on their way and decipher the 'blind' letters, those with a street but no town or misheard place names: 'Warsaw' for Walsall'; 'Persia' for 'Pershore' or a classic error 'Arijaba' when what was meant was 'Harwich Harbour.'

AROUND THE WORLD

"Maisons Speciales"

The Paris Council has come to the decision to close all the 'Maisons Speciales' across the Seine Department of Paris. The closure of the licensed brothels was given overwhelming support when proposed by a woman councillor, who formerly worked within the French Resistance movement. The system which gave France a special reputation within Western Europe, was advocated and utilised by the Nazi occupiers and their Vichy sympathisers. There are, however, still those who support the network, and some Councillors have since received offers of bribery to keep them open.

Emile Litters 'Aladdin' will be the only one 'true' pantomime among the Christmas plays in the London West End this year, due to the shortages of theatre space. Theatres are making such good business since the relaxation of war restrictions that they are packed to capacity every night and booked for weeks in advance, leaving pantomime impresarios without a space to perform.

The origins of the pantomime can be found as early as the 16th Century, from Italian entertainment, where evidence of stock characters of a similar vain to modern day pantomimes can be found in their theatres. By the 18th Century, this theatre had developed and migrated to London's stages, where early pantomimes told classical stories using the original Italian stock characters. The Harlequin became the star of London pantomime, and the first London Harlequin, John Rich, used his fortune to construct the Covent Garden Theatre, now a prominent feature of London theatre. 'Harlequinades', love stories full of slapstick humour and mimed to music, dominated the pantomime for over 100 years, until the Drury Lane Theatre implemented a speaking Harlequin and started writing pantomimes based on old English folk stories. Dick Whittington, Robin Hood and the Children of the Wood became household stories through theatre, and soon domestic culture and satire became a key theme of the pantomime, a theme which attracted a lot of enjoyment.

The Victorian Pantomime, as this became known, changed the industry forever. Gone were mimes and classic stories, in favour of satire and slapstick, with the retention of a now stock character of a women authority figure played by a man.

IN THE NEWS

Monday 24   **"Search for Scots"** Over 1,000 applications for news of their Scottish ancestors have flooded in from all corners of the globe following preliminary meetings of the Scottish Ancestry Research Council.

Tuesday 25   **"Christmas at Peace"** The British public were treated to their first peacetime Christmas for six years, and spirits across the Country were high. Nevertheless, they were still forced to *'make a little go a long way'*.

Wednesday 26 **"A British Christmas in Germany"** Troops in the British Zone of Berlin and wider Germany were given the day off yesterday and today for Christmas celebrations. The officers served the mens' dinner in the traditional way.

Thursday 27   **"Coal Recruitment"** With supplies of coal dwindling, and an acute manpower shortage, the Minister of Fuel has appointed a Director of Recruitment for the coal mining industry.

Friday 28   **"Mine Disposal"** After strong gales hit the South Coast, two mines were washed up on forcing the mine disposal squad to descend a 400ft cliff to get to them.

Saturday 29   **"Surplus Wool Cloth"** Over 3,000 firms need to apply for membership of the 'Wool Industry Surplus Cloth Corporation' to ensure the orderly sale of government surplus.

Sunday 30   **"Military Peace-Time Tasks"** Whilst a large portion of the RAF has had a reduced role since the end of the war, Transport Command has been busier than ever orchestrating the demobilisation of troops on the continent.

Monday 31   **"No More Registration"** The Ministry of Education has announced the abolition of the compulsory registration for children up to the age of 16. The scheme was put in place to encourage young people to join youth organisations.

HERE IN BRITAIN

"Secrets of Pepperbox Hill"

Motorists living in and around Wiltshire are familiar with the steep hill climb up Pepperbox Hill, but few know of the secrets that lay hidden within. It was just a couple of years before the war that the Admiralty realised the vulnerability of leaving naval munitions on the ground, where they were susceptible to air attacks. Instead, several sites were earmarked for underground storage spaces, including Pepperbox Hill in West Dean. Thousands of tons of explosives were hidden within miles of tunnelled rock, transported by a narrow train track.

AROUND THE WORLD

"Food From New Zealand"

Rationing in New Zealand has reached new heights as cuts are necessary to allow the country to send Britain an extra 22,000 tons of meat and 14,000 tons of butter each year. The dominion's gifts to Britain don't end there however, as £75,000 in patriotic funds has been set aside to be put towards food, with 40,000 packages already prepared to be sent to hospitals and orphanages across Britain. Throughout the war, New Zealand provided Britain with two-thirds of its butter ration, one-third of its cheese, and one-seventh of its meat.

SPIRIDONOVKA PALACE

After almost 10 days of discussion and negotiation, the foreign ministers of Britain and the US are set to leave Moscow after the announcement confirming that a peace treaty had been agreed between the Allies and the former German satellites, came from the Kremlin. The foreign ministers were mainly at the Kremlin but talks would also have taken place in the Spiridonovka Palace.

This Palace was built by the eccentric Arseny Morozon, the younger son of a Moscow textile 'king'. Born into great wealth, he was uninterested in his father's business, instead engaging in a hedonistic life, indulging his greatest passions, hunting and dog-breeding. In the late 1890's he built a Gothic-Moorish castle next to his mother's classical mansion on Volkhonka Street, on a plot she offered him on his 25th birthday. Inspired by the faux-medieval Pena Palace in Portugal with an added façade copied from the House of Shells in Salmanca. The building provoked widespread ridicule even before it was completed, being absurdly out of place in central Moscow. Tolstoy, in his book 'The Resurrection' has a passer-by describe the building as a *'stupid unnecessary palace for a stupid useless person'.*

If the exterior was eccentric, the interior followed suit, reflecting an absolute eclecticism of styles. From pseudo-Gothic to Empire, Arabic to Chinese, the Palace is filled with carved woodwork, Persian carpets, marble mantelpieces, Empire furniture and stained glass. After the Revolution, the Palace became a theatre until 1928, then the embassy of different countries and even home to British newspapers. It is now the Reception House for the Soviet Foreign Minister. In the Music Room, where the meetings took place, hangs a painting presented by the British Government of Anthony Eden signing, in the presence of Churchill, Molotov and Maisky, the Anglo Soviet Treaty of May 1942.

1945 Calendar

January

S	M	T	W	T	F	S
	1	2	3	4	5	6
7	8	9	10	11	12	13
14	15	16	17	18	19	20
21	22	23	24	25	26	27
28	29	30	31			

February

S	M	T	W	T	F	S
				1	2	3
4	5	6	7	8	9	10
11	12	13	14	15	16	17
18	19	20	21	22	23	24
25	26	27	28			

March

S	M	T	W	T	F	S
				1	2	3
4	5	6	7	8	9	10
11	12	13	14	15	16	17
18	19	20	21	22	23	24
25	26	27	28	29	30	31

April

S	M	T	W	T	F	S
1	2	3	4	5	6	7
8	9	10	11	12	13	14
15	16	17	18	19	20	21
22	23	24	25	26	27	28
29	30					

May

S	M	T	W	T	F	S
		1	2	3	4	5
6	7	8	9	10	11	12
13	14	15	16	17	18	19
20	21	22	23	24	25	26
27	28	29	30	31		

June

S	M	T	W	T	F	S
					1	2
3	4	5	6	7	8	9
10	11	12	13	14	15	16
17	18	19	20	21	22	23
24	25	26	27	28	29	30

July

S	M	T	W	T	F	S
1	2	3	4	5	6	7
8	9	10	11	12	13	14
15	16	17	18	19	20	21
22	23	24	25	26	27	28
29	30	31				

August

S	M	T	W	T	F	S
			1	2	3	4
5	6	7	8	9	10	11
12	13	14	15	16	17	18
19	20	21	22	23	24	25
26	27	28	29	30	31	

September

S	M	T	W	T	F	S
						1
2	3	4	5	6	7	8
9	10	11	12	13	14	15
16	17	18	19	20	21	22
23	24	25	26	27	28	29
30						

October

S	M	T	W	T	F	S
	1	2	3	4	5	6
7	8	9	10	11	12	13
14	15	16	17	18	19	20
21	22	23	24	25	26	27
28	29	30	31			

November

S	M	T	W	T	F	S
				1	2	3
4	5	6	7	8	9	10
11	12	13	14	15	16	17
18	19	20	21	22	23	24
25	26	27	28	29	30	

December

S	M	T	W	T	F	S
						1
2	3	4	5	6	7	8
9	10	11	12	13	14	15
16	17	18	19	20	21	22
23	24	25	26	27	28	29
30	31					

Printed in Great Britain
by Amazon